M000187994

TRANSCENDING THE MIND:
SOME DISASSEMBLY REQUIRED!

HOW TO TAKE APART YOUR NOISY MIND

HELEN HAMILTON

BALBOA.PRESS

A DIVISION OF HAY HOUSE

Copyright © 2021 Helen Hamilton.

All rights reserved. No part of this book may be used or reproduced by any means, graphic, electronic, or mechanical, including photocopying, recording, taping or by any information storage retrieval system without the written permission of the author except in the case of brief quotations embodied in critical articles and reviews.

Balboa Press books may be ordered through booksellers or by contacting:

Balboa Press
A Division of Hay House
1663 Liberty Drive
Bloomington, IN 47403
www.balboapress.co.uk
UK TFN: 0800 0148647 (Toll Free inside the UK)
UK Local: 02036 956325 (+44 20 3695 6325 from outside the UK)

Because of the dynamic nature of the Internet, any web addresses or links contained in this book may have changed since publication and may no longer be valid. The views expressed in this work are solely those of the author and do not necessarily reflect the views of the publisher, and the publisher hereby disclaims any responsibility for them.

The author of this book does not dispense medical advice or prescribe the use of any technique as a form of treatment for physical, emotional, or medical problems without the advice of a physician, either directly or indirectly. The intent of the author is only to offer information of a general nature to help you in your quest for emotional and spiritual well-being. In the event you use any of the information in this book for yourself, which is your constitutional right, the author and the publisher assume no responsibility for your actions.

Any people depicted in stock imagery provided by Getty Images are models, and such images are being used for illustrative purposes only. Certain stock imagery © Getty Images.

Print information available on the last page.

ISBN: 978-1-9822-8336-0 (sc)
ISBN: 978-1-9822-8337-7 (e)

Balboa Press rev. date: 03/17/2021

CONTENTS

Dedication... vii

Chapter 1   Introduction 1
Chapter 2   Pathway of Mind and Understanding 5
Chapter 3   The Anatomy of a Mind Pattern 9
Chapter 4   The Practical Things to Know Before
            You Start 15
Chapter 5   Stage One: The Trigger Event................... 23
Chapter 6   Stage Two: The Inner Response............... 35
Chapter 7   Stage Three: The Emotional Charge 47
Chapter 8   Stage Four: The Assumptions of Mind....... 59
Chapter 9   Stage Five: The Belief in Separation...........73
Chapter 10 Stage Six: The Belief in Otherness.............87
Chapter 11 Stage Seven: The Belief in Becoming
            the Allness 99
Chapter 12 Conclusion 109

Appendix... 111

DEDICATION

This book is dedicated to all those who wish to wake up and to humanity as a whole. It will give you the tools to end suffering and to wake up fully. May your light shine in this world so brightly that no darkness may remain. This book is for you.

CHAPTER I

Introduction

Most of humanity is lost in the illusion that they are their minds; that whatever their mind says they must automatically believe, because it is them. We may say "my mind..." and "my thoughts..." but few of us can actually see that these are appearing in us and not actually what we are.

This book is offered so that we may finally and fully transcend the mind by understanding the actual process involved. Information about the process and how to move to the next stage helps us to soften our resistance because we begin to see that every awakened being has travelled the road we are on. Everyone must walk this path right to the end and nobody is exempt; not even the Buddha.

As human beings we evolve spiritually by learning new information, questioning its truth and then applying it. At the end of this process we become what we were previously reading about; we are the living Truth and not just holding it in our heads as more book knowledge. Our mind and body are always in a seeming process of becoming ever clearer, brighter and happier manifestations of the True Self. Our unmanifested nature is ever perfect, total and complete.

With this book you will be able to take any particular mind pattern that is happening for you right now, understand it, work it backwards and end up in the Awakened State as the perfection that you are.

This book is ground-breaking in that it brings together each stage of transcendence of the mind in clear steps that are easily explained. Examples of everyday events, their emotional and mental responses and how to use them to totally transcend the mind are also given. These examples are from real students as they are growing on the pathway.

As you are reading this book and applying what you learn, you will be able to check your progress by the examples and explanations in the book. Also, you will be able to assess your own progress through the feeling of release, opening and greater peace each time you progress to the next chapter.

The processes in this book are available to everyone; it does not matter whether you have done lots of spiritual practice before or none. The processes are applicable to anyone who has an interest in moving beyond their mind. You do not need to have any previous knowledge of spiritual traditions, cultures or the various pathways at all. In fact, this book may work best for those that are totally open and able to simply read, apply and transcend.

You are greatly encouraged to read all of the chapters in this book at least once. This is especially so, even if the first few chapters seem to be quite basic and you have advanced beyond them in your spiritual practice. This is because it will help you to see that at each stage there is a particular set of opposites or dualities to be transcended. You do not need to understand this, but reading the chapters in order will help your consciousness to understand the process it is going through and advance to the next level much more easily.

Transcending mind is like peeling away the layers of an onion and as you learn how to peel back each layer, you become more adept at the next one. The journey becomes quicker and easier even at the end with the small and possibly tricky layers. In the end you are left with Nothing inside the onion; the Formlessness or Awareness that you are and always were.

Transcending the mind is a journey from here to here. You already are this pure awareness but we must all peel back the layers of the mind that obscure the true light that we are and live as that experientially.

CHAPTER 2

Pathway of Mind and Understanding

There are many pathways to Truth or Awakening, such as the pathway of heart or through deep self-inquiry. Many pathways stress the importance of meditation and contemplation also. These are all very useful tools and are encouraged, although in this book we will be working with our mind to begin to understand the roots of our suffering and how to unravel it.

Each mind pattern we have is like a woven thread hanging loose from the garment of the mind or egoic sense of self. If we know exactly where to pull the thread, we can unravel the whole thing in a relatively short space of time. If we can begin to see that everyone has these patterns and that they are there to actually help you, then we will be much more confident and successful in letting them go.

The pathway of mind is really only a process of actually deeply taking a look at our mind and asking why it works the way it does. Understanding leads to acceptance which will in turn lead to dissolving the repetitive mind patterns that cause us so much suffering. Most of us spend our time consciously or unconsciously resisting our mind, wishing it would quieten down or stop altogether. This only serves to increase the noise it tends to make.

Please note that when I use the word "mind" or "ego" I mean the aspect of our mind which is somewhat dysfunctional, repetitive, doubting, judging and fearing etc. It is this aspect of our mind we would like to dissolve and transcend and not the useful, functional aspect of mind that reminds us that we have left the oven on or we are going to be late for work if we do not leave now. This healthy aspect of mind will still be available after you fully awaken to your True Self and live in, and as, the Freedom you are. In fact, you will be able to access your mind whenever you want or need to use it rather than being used by it.

This pathway will be particularly useful if you have an extremely noisy or overly analytical mind and find it challenging to sit and meditate. In this pathway we are using the faculties of the mind to aid in its own dissolution. Each person's mind already has the wish to come to rest as the Effortless Self and will do so when given the right information. Just like a tiny splinter of wood can go unseen in your finger for a long time and yet cause a great deal of pain, so too can the wrong ideas cause unrest and unease within your mind. It is like an itch you cannot scratch or a wound that keeps on opening and never fully heals.

All we are going to do in this book with these processes is to give the mind the ability to see what the wrong ideas are finally. With that information we can finally come to see what has been causing our pain and choose to move beyond it.

Follow each chapter and apply what you read completely and only move on to the next chapter when you feel an experiential shift has occurred and you feel a sense of openness or lightening in your being. This is very important because it will show you that you have transcended the particular level of consciousness around the particular mind pattern you are working on. As you apply the processes in the chapters on one mind pattern, you will begin to see how easily all the other patterns can dissolve too.

Making a Molehill Out of a Mountain

At first, the idea of undoing all these mind patterns can seem like a mountain to climb with no equipment. But as you begin to systematically undo each pattern it becomes faster and easier. Each time you transcend a barrier, belief or block you gain access to some energy that has been tied up in a loop so it gets quicker, easier and exponentially more powerful. It soon becomes obvious that if you undo a few mind patterns, then at some point the whole thing will collapse and there will be only silence and peace. You will come to see there is already peace and silence but it may appear to be hidden under the noise of the mind.

Each time you look at a mind pattern you will notice it is clearer, simpler and easier to see where your energy has been tied up in it. Each time you are clearer, more aware and much more powerfully focused. Each time you will be less distractible by the mind. At some point, like a house of cards, it will all collapse and you can simply be yourself without the inner journalist obsessively commenting on everything that happens to you.

You will begin to fall in love with the simplicity of this pathway and the ease of the steps that have a simple and logical process. You may also begin to fall in love with the reward of more peace, stillness and happiness for transcending each mind pattern. Our mind will tell us that it is total enlightenment or bust, that unless we let go of every single mind pattern then we will never be happy. On the contrary. What we will find is that each time we let go, each time we investigate a belief or question an assumption, we actually achieve a new level of consciousness. We will find that the effort is worth it and that we are living a happier life every time we apply this. There are immediate and tangible benefits to applying this and we may even find that we reach a stage that we are so happy that we do not care anymore about awakening or enlightenment!

From this point on, you will always have the tools within your grasp to handle anything that life throws at you; that is the greatest of all confidence.

Let's get started!

CHAPTER 3

The Anatomy of a Mind Pattern

In this chapter, we are going to start from the end and show the whole process. In this way our consciousness will already be starting to let go as we begin to feed it the correct information. In effect, we will see the whole road map for the territory we are going to cover so we know what to bring on the journey.

Below we lay out the stages of transcending a mind pattern (also called vasanas, or latent tendencies of the mind). I will describe each stage in general and then we will look at one stage in detail in the next chapters.

We will also take a quick look at the false idea we must still be believing at each stage.

Step One: The Trigger Event in the World

Something or someone acts or speaks in a certain way that causes an inner response within us of great emotion. We blame that person or circumstance for upsetting us and try our hardest to change them.

9

False Idea:

- I can change the outside world to get what I want and to make me feel better.

Step Two: The Inner Response

With a little inner searching we can come to see that the trigger event is not really what is upsetting: rather it is the inner response of repetitive, nonsense thoughts caused by the trigger that are causing us to suffer and we try to make it stop.

False idea:

- I can do something with these thoughts to make them go away. I can reject them or accept them.

Step Three: The Emotional Charge

In time we will come to see that both the trigger event and the inner response are "symptoms" of an underlying emotional charge from an emotion we have not allowed ourselves to feel as yet. We must allow ourselves the time and space to actually feel our emotions fully so that the energy of them may dissipate.

False Idea:

- If I don't allow myself to feel this emotion it will go away and I won't have to deal with it. Also, if I allow myself to feel this emotion it will overwhelm me.

Stage Four: The Assumptions of Mind

We can see in this stage that all negative emotions are the result of some deeply rooted beliefs about ourselves that we have not wanted to see consciously. These beliefs are thoughts that have been believed so often that we never question their truth anymore; they come from our environment, our programming and our karma.

False Idea:

* These beliefs about me are true and I am unworthy, guilty, not good enough or not safe. It is so painful to think about them that all I can do is bury them deep in my consciousness.

Stage Five: The Belief in Separation

In this stage we come to see that all these deep-rooted beliefs would not be possible if it were not for the fact that we firmly believe that we are a separate person or that we are this body and mind only. Only once we believe that we are the body can we pick up all these other beliefs as "mine". We begin to see that there really is only this one belief to work on to undo all of the mind's insanity.

False Idea:

* I really am a separate person, alone in time and space, making my way through life trying to survive. When this body dies so will I.

11

Stage Six: The Belief in Otherness

In this stage we may have seen many times that we are not really a separate person; rather that we are the formless awareness itself. Although we have seen this, we may not have fully digested the meaning of it and can still have a tendency to see other people, to relate to others as if they were separate too. We must begin to see that if we are not separate then neither are they.

False Idea:

- I am formless but other people are still real and separate, there is an end to my formlessness.

Stage Seven: The Belief in Becoming the Allness

Once we have seen that there are no "others" and nothing else than the Self, we may find ourselves alternating between feeling totally at home as the Self and occasionally moving back into identification with being a person. We will believe in the reality of the one that is learning to stay as the Self more and more of the time. We will believe that it takes some time to get back to the Self fully or to eliminate the remnants of a person.

False Idea:

- The illusion of there being anything other than Truth, than the Self, is real and it takes some time to completely dissolve it and be able to consciously stay as the Self only. Illusion or untruth must be eliminated and I can do something to make that happen.

Finally, we come to see that there is no time, no process, no transcendence or letting go of anything. There is no need for practice to "stay as the Self" as all *is* the Self. There is only the Allness that encompasses all illusion too. It is all the Self. At this point, the remainder of the dysfunctional mind will lose its grip and there will be great peace, love and joy.

CHAPTER 4

The Practical Things to Know Before You Start

In this chapter we will discuss a few practical things that are useful to know in this process. Knowing this information will allow you to progress much faster and use much less energy to question why things are happening at each stage. You will begin to see the patterns coming up more easily and look at them much more efficiently.

Resistance to Change

Firstly, it will help to know that at each stage the mind will put up resistance to try to stop you from seeing the truth. We must expect this and know how to deal with it in advance. Our mind is invested in keeping things as they are right now and if we understand why it resists change so much, then we can soften the resistance and stop fighting against it.

What we call our mind is really a collection of survival tendencies, conditioned responses and other habitual thoughts. Most of the traffic of thought is really monotonous and repetitive and rarely do we have access to new and unusual thoughts unless we are actively engaged on a pathway to awakening. We can understand this better by taking a look at what causes these repetitive thoughts.

Over eons of evolution, our animalistic or more primitive nature had to develop the ability to assess a situation carefully and clearly and make a decision almost immediately. Our brain had to decide in a few seconds whether something was a threat, an ally or perhaps something to try to mate with. Our ability to survive as primitive man often depended on making the correct decision to run or fight in a few seconds. Those that made the wrong decision perhaps did not live long enough to pass along those genes! In order to facilitate a speedy decision-making process, our brain catagorises things and labels them and uses these previously determined labels to instantly make a decision about something. We can imagine primitive man being bitten by a snake or poisonous spider and for the rest of his life he would avoid anything that looks like a snake or spider. We can even recognise this conditioning in our more modern brains; how many of us are scared of spiders for seemingly very little reason?

Over the generations of evolution this function has developed into a highly complex system of analysing and catagorising not only our physical environment but also our emotional and mental environment. We instantly label someone as nice because they make us feel happy, even though the opposite may be true. We also tend to regard anything that makes us feel physical, emotional or mental pleasure as good and anything that causes pain as bad. Of course, we do not have the space in this book to go through a psychological analysis of the human condition and how it developed. We can begin to see that each time we perceive something through our mind and think about it, we are actually not seeing the thing as it is but only seeing what we think about it after it's been run through our conditioning and programming.

What is the relevance of this to our pathway here in this book? Well, we can begin to see that if we begin to try something new and investigate directly the functioning of our mind patterns that we may meet with an automatic analysis of "new ways of doing things are bad" and "doing the same things again and again will produce new results". Of course, neither are ultimately true in every situation but we can begin to appreciate that such simple ideas as these might have been responsible for the survival of humanity as a primitive species, and as such these ideas are very much embedded in our consciousness and surface every time we try to change something.

We can all immediately recall a time when we tried to change a habit, to stop doing something, or start doing something, and we were met with great resistance and needed willpower. We can consider giving up smoking, losing weight or committing to a new exercise program and remember how it takes conscious effort to form a new habit or stop an old one.

Here in this book we are changing one simple habit of automatically believing certain thoughts and replacing it with the ability to assess whether believing these thoughts is still useful to us rather than blindly believing. If we can understand why this might be perceived as a threat at first to our mind, we can soften the resistance to the process and progress much faster and easier. We are pure awareness itself, the true Self of all, but we also always still have a human body and brain with all its conditioning that has kept us alive and helped us to reach this point. Consider where we would be without the simple conditioning of "crossing the road when traffic is coming is bad"! Don't fight the resistance to change when it appears; rather make an effort to understand it and you are already transcending it.

Gone or Not?

It will also help us to look at how we will actually experience the transcendence of each mind pattern. At each stage we can apply what we read in this book to a particular mind pattern and we will feel an experiential shift at some point. We will notice a sense of openness, lightness, relief or relaxation in the body once we have transcended a certain stage and it is the usual way of our mind to conclude that this mind pattern is completely gone now. We may even feel we have let it go or released it.

Whilst it is true that we are completely finished with that stage of that particular mind pattern, we must also recognise that when we are ready to proceed to the next level of our awakening, the same pattern will seem to re-appear from nowhere and present itself exactly as before. This cannot be true of course because we are releasing something each time we apply the knowledge in this book and the fact that the same pattern resurfaced again must be viewed as a sign of our success in transcending and not failure.

The usual way that most humans treat the resurfacing of a mind pattern in our spiritual growth is to question whether we have even succeeded at all and to view it as a personal failure. If we can instead begin to see the pattern is presenting itself again due to our success, then we can proceed much faster. Consider how we cut down a tree that is threatening our property or land because of its size. We might first climb the tree to cut off the smaller branches and then we are able to cut back the main branches. After some time, we can then cut back the main trunk of the tree and finally we will treat the stump and remove it from the ground. At each stage we are working on the same tree and we might even question why we cannot simply save time and effort by cutting the root first.

Often, we need to work backwards to the root and remove big branches that might damage property if we simply cut the root. Transcending a mind pattern is like this in many ways and we can see that these "branches" are the way the mind pattern is showing itself in the world, in emotional ways and in familiar ways of thinking. Finally, we can cut the root of the pattern by seeing if we are not a separate person we would not have to even work on this pattern at all.

We must begin to regard the reappearance of a particular pattern with excitement rather than negativity and realise we are about to make another leap in our level of consciousness.

The Evidence of Our Success-
The Art of Contemplation

In this journey we are going to move beyond the noise of our mind and live in and as the peace itself. As such, we must be sure that we do not stop at the wrong place in our transcendence. Transcending the mind is achieved by contemplating a particular thought or belief pattern that we may have and asking openly and honestly if it is actually true. When we believe a thought, we are in fact saying "this is true for me" and automatically then, we must experience the effects of that belief.

An example might be that we can never get ahead in our job, that we will always be passed over for promotion opportunities. If we continue to believe the same thought then we are bound to live the same experience over and over, as reality has no option but to manifest itself in the way we expect. In transcending this belief, we will begin to question the assumptions and false ideas here and see if they are really true. We might question if it is true that we are not in control of job or promotion opportunities. We might come to see that it does not need to be true for us any longer and that the less we blindly believe that "these things always happen to me" then we can begin to move forward in this area.

The art of contemplation is to persist in our questioning until we see and feel an experiential shift in our level of consciousness. That means that we must not be fooled and accept a thought answer or an emotional answer. Here, we must be wiser than the mind and notice the sequence or levels of answer we will receive. At first when we contemplate, we must ask an open question such as "is it really true that...." and we will have a thought answer appear first. Usually we receive an answer that goes something like "well of course it's true because I keep seeing it happen in my life". As we persist with our sincere and open wish to see if this belief is actually true (and not just presumed to be) we will begin to receive different thought answers such as "maybe it's only been true because I believed it" or "maybe it has never been true but I have put my attention on it long enough that it had to show up".

As more and more of these new thought answers come, we will move to the second stage of contemplation which is usually some sort of emotional answer. We will begin to feel more positive and optimistic, we will feel that we have a choice now to change our path, we will feel happier in general. This is a breakthrough but we must not stop here. We must continue to ask the questions until not only do we experience a different manifestation (i.e. a better job offer) but also an experiential shift in our awareness. It is vital to see that our contemplation is not complete until we feel we have let go of something, released a burden or we feel lighter or more expansive.

Another way we will notice that a shift in our level of consciousness has occurred will be that the trigger event no longer pushes our buttons and creates an emotional response. The very same event can happen but we remain at peace inside. If we are to transcend the mind, we cannot accept a mind answer *or* an emotional answer. Emotions are the results of the thoughts we believe and are not reliable enough evidence that we have moved beyond a particular mind pattern. More positive emotions are a good sign that we are on the way to letting this go finally but not the end goal.

What we have just described is how to effectively use your mind to transcend your mind. Mind asks the question and the final answer is when the question no longer is relevant, it will be so obvious to you that it is not true, nor has it ever been. You believed a thought so it appeared to be true as you experienced it.

We must come to always and only accept a shift in our consciousness as an indication we have been successful in our contemplation. This is the key to moving beyond the reach of the mind once and for all. Accepting mind answers will only lead to more things that need questioning!

21

So, let's get started looking at each stage in more detail. We will describe how the stage will present itself in our lives and then we will look at the false idea that is sustaining it. We will then discover how to move beyond this false idea and into greater peace. Finally, we will back up what we have learned by looking at several real-life examples and applying this to them. We will end this process by having the knowledge, courage and insight to finally move beyond anything that has held us back.

CHAPTER 5

Stage One: The Trigger Event

What is a Trigger Event?

We have all had experiences in our life where someone says something to us and we feel an immediate and almost involuntary emotional response and we feel compelled to act in a certain way. We can be "triggered" by words spoken to us, about us, or even a lack or presence of something. Consider the last time you did not have enough time or money to do what you wanted or needed to do; remember for a moment the last time you had an argument with your partner. As humans, most of us live a life where we feel pulled around by life and are bound to ride the waves of mental and emotional stress caused by these trigger events. We may even find once the trigger has gone that we still cannot leave the situation and thoughts are still raging like a storm happening inside our head.

Most of us have no choice but to be triggered and have the same involuntary response of strong emotion, stress, and to continue the loop over and over. Even when we might be aware that we're being triggered we have no idea how to break this cycle. We can find ourselves hurting others with our words and actions that come from a highly emotionalised place but are unable to stop it. We can feel like a puppet on a string. Most of humanity has only one option to try to break free, and that is to try to change or stop the trigger event itself. We may talk to the person that upsets us or try to reason with them, avoid them or many other actions.

We try to take action to change our life and the harder we try the more it seems to backfire and make the situation worse. Any action that we take is usually only perpetuating the cycle we are stuck in but we may not know that. It is fruitless to spend energy and time trying to get others to change to suit us. We may quickly find that we cannot rely on others to make us happy by acting in certain ways or by ceasing to act a particular way.

Transcending the False Idea

The way to transcend these trigger moments and gain back a sense of choice as to how we react to other people and events is simply to notice that we have a choice. We may not have realised as yet that the way we have been trying to fix these situations is not working and all our efforts to make something change to make us happier can only work temporarily at best, if at all.

We must realise that these trigger events AND the action we take to get rid of them is not effective because we cannot make someone change or cause something to shift in our outside world simply by effort alone.

The false idea in this stage is "**I can change the outside world to get what I want and to make me feel better**".

This is simply not true. We must learn to work on an inner level to cause lasting change. We must be able to accept that these things are happening because we are believing something that is not true.

Only by accepting that this is not true can we retrain ourselves to look inwards for the answer we seek. We finally can come to see that the world "out there" is only a reflection of our inner level of consciousness in each area. We may have a lower insight level for some areas of our life than others. We may be relaxed and open around finances with an "easy come and easy go" type of attitude, but when it comes to romance we may still believe that we have to go through many heartbreaks to find our soulmate.

Let's now look at real life examples from students to show how to transcend this stage:

Example 1 — Sarah used to get very angry and upset because her step mum has lied about her and Sarah found out. Sarah knew the lies were not true but she could not stop getting angry and reacting even though it didn't help and often only made things worse. She was worried that other people might believe the things that were being said about her.

In the past, Sarah tried to talk to her step mum and convince her that she should not be telling lies about her. Her words went unheard because her step mum was so used to lying that she did not even realise she was still doing it. Sarah had also tried to tell her friends and family that the lies were not true, but she ended up feeling like she was the one trying to cover up a guilty conscience rather than telling the truth.

Sarah would spend most of the time feeling angry, having disturbed sleep and higher stress levels. She would feel as though she just had to live with it and accept it even though it felt extremely unfair.

Upon realising that only taking action in the outside world to try and make the situation go away was not enough, Sarah was able to see the false idea that she can change her world to suit her better was actually holding her back. When she realised that her outer world was a reflection of what she was on the inside, she began to look at where she was not being true to herself. She began to see where she was not being authentically Sarah. This gave her a new-found sense of power and control over her life and a sense of integrity.

Sarah began to see that from this place she could speak to her step mum with a sense of authority that was not present before and she noticed that people began to respond to her differently. Although she still felt triggered by her step mum at first, she was much more able at let it go faster and eventually, Sarah came to see that people formed their opinions of her based on what she did and said and not by anything her step mum might have said about her.

Example 2 — Michael used to get very upset when people said he was very much like his father. Michael and his father have not always had a good relationship, and the idea that he was like his father was upsetting to him. He would always feel angry and disempowered when people said it. He felt that he was doomed to continue to become more and more like his dad as the years went by.

Michael tried to talk to the people that had said these things to ask them not to say them; he also had tried to eliminate the character traits that his dad had passed down to him. He felt he had worked hard on himself to be independent of his father and was "his own man". When he noticed that he was doing something that his dad would have done, or saying something like he remembered his dad saying, Michael would stop and try to do something different. He even found himself really doing things that he didn't find interesting just to appear to be different from his dad.

Michael felt that he could not be himself and that he would turn more into his dad as time went on. He watched his father complain, worry and fret over many things and could only see a bleak future for himself. Whatever he tried to do to escape from his father's shadow only seemed to bring him closer.

Once Michael saw the false idea he was believing he began to rethink how to deal with this. He began to remember that what people think about him and how he acts, is really only a reflection of their own thoughts and projections about Michael and NOT the same as what he is actually like. Michael began to look inside for the trigger and notice when it was happening. Over time he started to notice that sometimes people were comparing him to his father over positive traits. He began to notice there were many things about his father that he liked as well as those he did not like. Michael came to see that he had inherited positive and negative traits, ways of doing things and much from both his parents and that he had a choice. He was now free to keep the positive ones and not act out the negative ones. He began to see that even the things he had labelled as negative were actually helping him define more clearly what he wanted to be. Over time Michael came to see that a parent has no option but to pass along the positive and the negative and that it was in fact an opportunity to grow beyond what he was before. Now, Michael began to see that people compared him with his father when he did something positive or helped someone. Long buried memories of his childhood began to surface and Michael saw that his relationship with his father had not always been so traumatic for him and that there had been many times when he had looked up to his father as a role model.

Example 3 — Sally found herself frustrated, angry and tired because her neighbour's dog kept barking over and over. Her neighbours seemed to be out a lot and the dog would whine most of the time. Sally felt sorry for the dog but also angry as she could not have any peace at all. Sometimes the dog would bark all night too, and even when it was not barking, somehow Sally could not relax knowing it would soon bark again. What had started off as being simply a little annoyance and irritation had now become a major issue for Sally; she couldn't relax in her own home and had come to dread the sleepless nights.

Sally had tried to talk to her neighbours who were very unresponsive and she even found herself a little scared of the dog. She had contacted the police who told her to keep a record of when she was awakened and disturbed by the dog but still she could not relax. Sally had spoken to other neighbours and it seemed the dog was disturbing others on the street as well. Eventually, Sally noticed her neighbours with the dog were moving after several warnings from the police about noise disturbances. New people moved into the same house, and Sally noticed to her dismay they brought a large dog with them! Eventually, Sally chose to move, deciding that this must simply be a dog-friendly neighbourhood and that there was nothing she could do.

She carried with her a knot of tension in her gut and a longing for a good night's sleep.

When Sally came to understand she was at the effect of believing this false idea she vowed to change her methods. She began to see where she could look inwards for an inner disturbance that must be present. The barking dog was an outer reflection of something inside disturbing her. Sally noticed several times she could sit down and have a peaceful moment when the dog was not barking but she had ended up on Facebook or watching something on television instead of honouring her own time alone. She set aside a small place in one room of her house where it was "quiet time" and knew she could sit there and there would be no disturbance. She began to honour her own time alone and value the peace.

Sally noticed that her new neighbourhood seemed to be cat-friendly and even found that when she sat in her quiet corner, the neighbour's cat seemed to like to come and sit on her lap by coming through an open window. Often Sally would not even notice the cat was with her because she had fallen into a very deep meditation. Sally was still wary of dogs but could see that her outer world had changed to reflect her new found sense of value. Peace was one thing she could easily give herself and she vowed to do so.

Example 4 — David never seemed to have enough money no matter what he did. He had debt and struggled to pay his bills each month. He felt that no matter how hard he worked he could not seem to get ahead, and even when he did manage to earn some extra money, an unexpected bill would come and he was right back to where he started. David lived in a constant state of anxiety and stress over money.

Every time he struggled to pay a bill he felt that he should be doing more somehow and would feel guilty that he could not provide better for his family. He was afraid that he would lose control of his finances and worried about the effect on his health. Deep down he also wished that life could be easier. It did not seem to make sense the way it was.

David tried getting an extra job which helped for a while, but the interest on his debts ate up the extra money. He borrowed money from a few places to pay debts but in doing so only ended up in more debt. No matter how hard he tried, he seemed to be slowly sinking into an ever-worsening situation.

Once David saw that his actions had been coming from a weakened place due to believing the false idea that he could change his outside world, he began to make a change. He started to realise that financial abundance was not so much about the amount of hours worked but his beliefs around money that were holding him back. He began to open to miracles coming in and realised that alongside working for a living, he could also let himself be helped by the universe. David began to see that his finances were a reflection of his belief that everything we have comes from hard work and effort and he set about changing that. He noticed that his work started changing too; he was much more appreciated and was offered a promotion with better hours and an increased salary. He got to spend more time with his family and had more money. David really took to heart that an inner shift seemed to cause more money to come in, than any amount of hard work.

Whilst David was not rich in worldly terms, he knew that he was indeed abundant financially; he had changed his definition of abundance and now knew hoarding lots of money was not necessarily the way. He began to see there was a flow to money and once he figured out how to stay tuned into the flow he would always have enough somehow. David became happier, more relaxed and had much more energy from ceasing to worry. He could finally allow himself to be looked after.

Example 5 — Jenny had always been an outgoing type of person but had started to stay home much more often because she would often feel extremely tired and low when she had been around others. Jenny had tried all kinds of things to help her feel better but nothing seemed to work. She had tried protecting her energy with meditation, only seeing people that she felt were uplifting, cleansing her aura, wearing crystals and much more, but nothing seemed to change the fact that some people seemed inclined to dump their emotional and mental baggage on her.

Lately, Jenny could not even handle being around her family as they sometimes seemed so negative. No matter how much sleep Jenny got or what foods she avoided, nothing seemed to help. She felt as though she didn't even know which emotions she felt were hers and what had been absorbed from those around her. She began to dread public places such as supermarkets, train stations and airports and found them quickly overwhelming. Jenny felt isolated and unable to reach out to others for help because spending time with anyone seemed to cause her to have an "energetic hangover" that sometimes lasted for days.

Finally, Jenny saw the truth that she could not do anything to avoid this problem and the only way to solve this was to look inside. It was clear that anything she had tried to help herself was only making the situation worse. The more she had isolated herself and avoided negative people the worse the impact they had upon her when she had to see them such as at work or family gatherings. Jenny took a leap of faith and began to look inwards for what might be draining her energy and saw a few places in her life where she was not honouring her own needs at all. She began to make some changes and gave herself more time in nature to recharge herself. Jenny stopped working overtime all the time, having decided it was not worth the extra money to come home exhausted and depleted. With these changes and more, Jenny began to realise that nobody could affect her energy unless she believed it to be so. She began to feel happiness, relief and a sense of freedom that had replaced the trapped feeling and panic that she often felt. She saw that people's energy had such an effect on her because she felt deep down to be unsafe and vulnerable.

Amazingly Jenny found that some of the most negative people in her workplace were moving for various reasons. She met a new colleague at work who also liked to meditate and she felt uplifted again. Jenny never forgot that her energy was her own and only when she was at the effect of the belief that "people, places and things out there can hurt me" would she be bound to experience that in her life over and over.

It is important to note that in these examples action was still sometimes taken in the world "out there" even after transcending the false idea and that when we take action from a place of truth it will be much more effective at achieving the results we want to see. We must not fall into a trap of believing that ONLY the inner work is the key.

Sometimes from our place of transcendence we will be asked to take some action, speak up for ourselves or do the right thing and our actions will come from a higher place inside us. We may find ourselves much more able to do and say the right thing for ourselves and the other people involved that creates a win-win situation. Action taken from the lower level of consciousness often leaves a winner and a loser and only perpetuates the situation and trigger event cycle.

Conclusion

As you begin to see ever more clearly where you have been trying to change your world "out there" to make you feel better, you will feel more empowered. You will be able to take back your control and stop wasting effort and energy on ineffective action that produces very little results. The cause of all change is an inner shift of consciousness and the outer worldly change is only a symptom of this shift. We must continue to examine our lives and apply this knowledge in a specific way; for example, we can question the truth of many things we might have believed before. We can ask:

"Is it really true that I have to work hard for a living?"

"Is it really true that I meet all the wrong type of guys?"

"Is it really true that anything can affect me without my permission?"

We can apply the instruction provided in the previous chapter to contemplate the validity of such beliefs and begin to move beyond them. It is important to note that we have not transcended this stage until we feel a shift in our level of consciousness. Keep contemplating these questions until you feel that happen.

CHAPTER 6

Stage Two: The Inner Response

When we begin to contemplate along our journey, we may begin to see that it is not in fact the trigger event itself that has caused us to suffer but rather the response of the mind. We may begin to remember a time when the trigger event happened but caused us no stress at all. We can also notice that the same trigger can happen to other people and they have no resulting emotional and mental response. In addition to this, we can even come to notice that the things that trigger other people have no effect upon us; we may even question why somebody would get upset over something that means so little to us yet seems to matter a great deal to them.

From our questioning we can come to see that the trigger and the resulting emotional and mental barrage that we feel are not necessarily bound to happen together. We know there are things in our life that once bothered us but now we have let them go they no longer affect us. In short, we can come to see that we are really struggling because of the thoughts and emotions that come up when we are triggered and not by the trigger event itself.

This is really good news for us spiritually, because if it was the trigger event itself that was causing us pain, then we are bound to suffer it over and over, because we have no control over what happens in the world. Once we realise that we are suffering from the mental tirade of thoughts that plague our peace, then we can begin to tackle this another way. Let's look at the false idea that needs to be transcended in this stage.

Transcending the False Idea

The idea that needs to be transcended in this stage is relatively simple to see and transcend once we can accept that it is the thoughts about the trigger event that are bothering us and not the event itself.

False idea:

- If I resist these thoughts they will go away. I can make the thoughts stop or go away if I don't want them.

When we are triggered by something in our world, we can begin to slow down a little and see that 3 things are actually happening at the same time:

1. The trigger event occurs
2. Thoughts about the trigger events begin to happen in abundance
3. There is a quiet but automatic rejection of these thoughts and something that wants to push them away.

The key to transcending this stage is relatively simple. We can begin to question whether there is any truth in this idea. We can ask if there really is anything we need to do to get rid of these thoughts. Is this strategy effective? Is it actually working — to push them away? Or could there be a better way?

In time we will come to see that we are the one that is watching the thoughts; that at all times there is a silent witness to the thoughts and that witness is not a thought, nor is it thinking. If we can begin to digest this revelation then we gain back our power, because we can simply watch the thoughts that arise and we do not even need to reject them or accept them.

More importantly we can begin to notice that the rejecting or accepting of these thoughts is not really anything we can change. It is a biological or psychological process that goes on in our brain and we cannot change it. Some thoughts we like and want to pay attention to; others we do not like and want to ignore. We can simply sit back metaphorically and watch the thoughts come and go AND the urge to accept or reject them.

In time we may even come to see that the accepting or rejecting of these thoughts caused by a trigger event is actually a thought itself. There is simply a thought appearing that says "I don't want these thoughts" or "I like these thoughts and want more of them". We can just be the witness of these thoughts too and need do nothing about them. They will go just as quickly as they came.

Let's take a look again at our examples from students to illustrate how to move beyond this stage:

Example 1 — Sarah reflected on this stage of her journey and came to see that there had been times where people

37

had lied about her and it had not bothered her. She also could admit within herself that she had also lied about somethings in her past too and had been able to forgive herself for that. It began to be clear that it was the thoughts that the lies seemed to produce inside her that caused her unhappiness. She noticed that when she thought about her step mum there would be lots of thoughts coming all at once and even more when she thought about the lies.

In a moment of quiet reflection Sarah saw that she was trying to reject these thoughts somehow. She realised she had not perhaps appreciated the lack of thoughts and the quiet until something had triggered this barrage of thoughts. She began to question if it is really true that these thoughts can upset her and what, if anything, did she need to do about them?

Over time Sarah came to see that she was witnessing all of it. She could simply watch the lies being told about her. She could also watch the emotional and mental reaction inside herself that came. At first when it would happen she still felt an urge to do something about the thoughts and had to remain consciously as only a witness to it all. The first few times that Sarah applied this process the thoughts got stronger and more intense but she held her ground and just watched. In a short while the thoughts began to subside and the energy around them dissipated. It was as if somehow Sarah had been unknowingly fuelling it all by wanting to stop the thoughts.

Sarah began to witness more and more of her thoughts and felt an underlying sense of peace that was growing. She also felt encouraged and empowered that no matter what her mind told her, she could simply watch it come and go. This revelation was so powerful to Sarah and she noticed that witnessing the thoughts was hard to do at first, but amazingly enriching and empowering. She felt at peace most times even with a whole load of thoughts going on and she noticed that the more she simply watched her mind the less it began to make noise. She felt calmer in general and happier, more able to take effective action when things were not going her way.

Example 2 — Michael began to contemplate why he suffered each time someone compared him to his father, as it had begun to affect him again after his first seeing. He came to see he could not be upset by the thing itself but rather it was the thoughts about Michael not being true to himself that bothered him. When people compared Michael to his father he began to think that he would never achieve anything original and would only ever end up being a carbon copy of his father.

Michael noticed he had an ability to simply watch these thoughts. He also noticed that the more he watched them come and go the faster they actually left. In one strange moment Michael saw clearly that there was indeed a relationship between HOW he watched the thoughts and how much he suffered from them. This was an amazing epiphany for Michael because he realised that if he ONLY watched them with no intention for them to stay or go, then they left quickly! He also noticed that he did not get so emotional around the thoughts either. It was almost as if the desire to have a quiet mind was driving the noisy mind to make more noise! Michael also began to see that he was not the one watching with this desire, this interest in making it all stop. He saw that he was the one who could ONLY witness.

All else was just another thought such as "I want this to stop" or "It should not be this way".

Immediately upon seeing that Michael was only witnessing he felt peaceful no matter what occurred. He felt calm and content and knew he was empowered by his realisation. He knew now that his most natural state of being was simply to watch and began to witness more and more areas of his life.

Example 3 — Once Sally began to ponder her situation more deeply she began to notice that there had been many times when she had fallen asleep for a nap during the day even with the neighbour's dog barking. She started to see that it could not actually be the dog itself that was keeping her awake and she became more aware of the tension of thoughts and emotional charge that built up when this happened. In time Sally began to see that it was the thoughts that made her feel tension, wired and unable to sleep, for as soon as the dog started barking she would have thoughts of "here we go again" and "I am going to be so tired tomorrow at work if I don't sleep tonight". She noticed some energy within her that wanted to just stop the whole thing, thoughts included and simply pretend it never happened.

A question began to arise inside Sally and she became curious what would happen if she simply had no opinion about the dog barking or the thoughts it seemed to cause. Deep inside Sally felt she was really onto something. She waited impatiently for the next time the dog began to bark and along came all the usual thoughts. She imagined that her brain was a computer and simply allowed these programmes to run on their own. What Sally experienced was very different to the other times, because as soon as she welcomed these thoughts she began to feel calm, relaxed and the tension began to lift. Sally realised quite quickly that her inability to sleep during these moments was not due to the dog at all or even the thoughts! It was caused by her own closing off and trying to shut down her mind! This was an amazing epiphany for Sally when she absorbed it fully because it put her back in control of her life and wellbeing. She began to test it every time her mind was running along on its own train of thought by simply letting it happen. The more she relaxed the more her mind relaxed. For the first time ever that Sally could remember, she woke up the next morning and realised that she had fallen asleep and slept all night, even though her mind was very busy as she lay down on the pillow. Sally realised that she had firmly believed that she needed to clear her mind in order to be able to relax or sleep and this was obviously not true for her anymore.

Example 4 — David began contemplating the ideas he had about money and noticed a few significant things; he saw that he had firmly believed that "money does not grow on trees" and that "we have to work hard for money". He saw that when the trigger event happened in his life, it seemed to activate all these thoughts in various ways. He had many thoughts about how long it would take to pay his debts back and even noticed that having debt made him feel inadequate in some way.

David decided to try a new approach when these thoughts were triggered. He began to have a new attitude to these thoughts when they came up and he wanted to test it out. One day when David went to the cash machine, his account had much less in it than he was expecting. Immediately a panic rose within him and he began to worry how he was going to pay his remaining monthly bills. He found himself getting angry that he hadn't paid more attention to the situation and then irritated that he felt out of control. He also felt humiliated that people behind him in the queue to use the machine had seen him walk away with no cash. He decided enough was enough and walked back to his car in a cloud of anger and worry. He sat in the car in the quiet and simply waited for his mind to begin its normal punishing routine of thoughts and decided upon his new mantra. "What am I going to do now? How am I going to manage?" said his mind. "I don't know but it will be ok" came the words out of David's mouth. He started laughing in that moment because he saw that something already knew it would be ok. He had been in this position many times and yet knew something must be looking after him.

"How am I going to explain this to the family?" said his mind and immediate response was "I don't know but it will be ok". David felt a sense of relief as he realised it really would be ok somehow. A strange realisation came upon him that maybe it wasn't all his responsibility to fix this at all! Yes of course he would work hard and do what he could but what if this was a test of his trust and faith that life would look after him? A smile appeared on his lips and he relaxed a little in his seat. He noticed this idea gave him a lot of relief and power back. He ended up sitting in the car for over 30 minutes while he just watched the thoughts come and go, the questions and accusations from his mind came over and over about how he was "not very good at money" and each time he simply agreed and said it would be ok. He knew that nothing had actually changed in his world and yet somehow he felt empowered, confident and back in control. He was sure he had somehow stumbled upon a major key to getting out of this mess altogether.

Tears ran down his face as it dawned upon David that he had it all backwards. He suddenly KNEW with all his being that the lack of money was only a symptom of an illness inside him and that the illness was his allowing this self-punishment to occur. The feelings, thoughts and lack of money came from this and not the other way around! He began to notice that somehow, somewhere in his past he had appointed himself as sole caretaker financially for his entire life and family and that was an unreasonable burden for him to carry. No wonder he could not live up to that and no wonder he felt a failure.

David drove home and sat talking with his wife for hours. Sometimes he laughed and sometimes he cried but he was a changed man from that day on. If a lack of money occurred for him he no longer needed to accept his mind's judgement that this equalled him being a failure at life; it was simply a lack of money and nothing else.

Example 5 — Jenny had spent time contemplating her challenges around being with other people and feeling drained. She felt as though she had moved beyond it with the discovery that it was the inner response to the situation that was causing her issues, rather than the people themselves, but nonetheless the issue seemed to be returning again. More and more she felt the need to isolate herself again and stay at home. She realised there must now be something else to see and understand regarding this. She thought about it and realised if it was not the outside world that was affecting her energy and she was still suffering then she must not be dealing with the inner response to it as effectively.

Jenny began to examine what happened when she was triggered and she noticed a lot of thoughts coming up that were bringing fear, worry and doubt as to whether she could have a normal life. Her mind would tell her that she would never be able to live a full social life again and that she would always be a loner. This made Jenny feel so bad she would try to ignore these thoughts and many other similar ones. She realised that by avoiding interaction with other people she had really been avoiding the thoughts about those people! Maybe that was the real issue and it never was about the energy of others! Jenny began to see that the avoidance of anything did not really feel true and that pushing these thoughts away was causing her to lose a lot of energy. The more Jenny looked at this the more empowered she began to feel again.

Jenny sat down and contemplated the thoughts and began to question them. She realised they persisted and came back because she was trying to reject them constantly. It was almost as if the thoughts were asking to be heard; simply to be heard. Could it be that simple? Jenny began to simply listen to the thoughts and vowed not to do anything with them. Amazingly jenny found the thoughts lost all power to make her feel bad when she was only listening to them. When she felt that they were true or that they meant something to her they caused a great deal of negative emotions again very quickly. Jenny began to experiment with believing the thoughts and then switching back to just listening and noticed that it really was her choice to be affected by the thoughts or not. The very moment she took these thoughts to be true, she felt weak, drained and out of control of her energy. Jenny was shocked at how quickly this had an effect but it was easily undone because the moment she began to see them as "just thoughts" she noticed her energy coming back and the thoughts could not stay.

In time Jenny began to see that it is really resisting thoughts that causes us to lose our power, emotional and mental energy and that it is a choice how we deal with our thoughts. She also saw that two very different paths lay ahead for her and most importantly she had a choice.

Conclusion

For each trigger event in our lives, we can begin to write a list of the common thoughts that come to us when the trigger happens. Notice the ones that you seem to automatically believe and experiment with simply letting them be there. You can ask yourself "is it true I have to believe or resist these thoughts?" or "Is it true I have to push them away?" As you begin to try a different approach with any thoughts that come repetitively and simply be a witness to them, you will find yourself gaining back power and confidence in your abilities. This will bring joy back to your life because you will realise that no matter how your mind bombards you for the rest of your life, you will have the tools to simply witness the thoughts and allow them to pass. Never again need you be at the mercy of a relentlessly noisy mind that may seem to be insisting upon punishing you.

CHAPTER 7

Stage Three: The Emotional Charge

Before we take a look at the next layer of each mind pattern, let's remind ourselves that although we have had breakthroughs at each stage, it is very likely that the mind pattern will return again. The trigger will begin to bother you again at each stage when you are ready to transcend further. This will happen because you are destined to fully transcend your mind and as such it will push you all the way to awakening or enlightenment. We must be mature in our attitude and be ready and welcoming when these same patterns resurface and not look at them in a negative way.

Each step along the way gets easier to see and faster to transcend because you are gaining more of your power back by being your True Self more and more. You are not a person, you are the formless awareness and you are already beyond the mind. This book is just helping you to peel back the layers of the mind so you can see ever more clearly what you already are.

In Stage 3 we come to see that the trigger event AND the thoughts that occur are really not the cause of our struggle. We can start to see that even if we witness the thoughts they still may keep coming and we have to work on a deeper level.

The thoughts are being produced and the trigger event has to manifest in our life because we have suppressed emotions that have built up over our lifetime and we have not allowed this emotional charge to be felt and dissipated.

Only by allowing ourselves to notice the emotions behind the thoughts and fully feel them, will the thoughts ever truly subside. The thoughts are attracted to emotional build-up of energy and are not the true cause.

In order to do this we must take responsibility for our emotions and learn that it's ok to feel them. Perhaps in our life nobody has actually shown us how to handle such intense emotions and we have had only a few options to cope with them so we usually suppress them or project them onto others. At some point in this process of waking up to our true nature we must become willing to feel these emotions. We need not feel them all at once but we do have to change our tactics without shame. Nearly all adults have really very little skills at dealing with emotions and it seems to be our way to try to ignore them or hope they will go away. Even when we have felt emotions we are usually seeing it as a sign of weakness.

Transcending the False Ideas

There are two main false ideas that have held us captive in this stage:

1. If I don't allow myself to feel this emotion it will go away and I won't have to deal with it.

2. Also, if I allow myself to feel this emotion it will overwhelm me and it will be unpleasant or I will not be able to shut it off again.

Notice that both of these ideas are your mind's way of avoiding having to feel the emotions. Our mind is trying to perpetuate its survival mechanisms and it thinks that if we feel the emotions and they go, that the mind will collapse and be non-existent. To some degree that's true, as the thoughts will be no longer produced due to the backlog and build-up of emotional charge, but we will still be able to use our mind when we need it for a functional purpose. We will still be able to plan an event, write a shopping list or get to work on time. Most of the resistance at this stage will come because your mind fears its own end. Once you know this is not true, you can push through the resistance and feel the emotions anyway.

One key factor that makes transcending this level quick and easy is to ensure you put all your attention on the emotion once it comes up. To do this, we must notice that thoughts come first usually but then we can sense the emotion underneath that is asking to be felt. If we keep attention on our thoughts we are in fact still suppressing the emotion. This is vital to understand fully because it is not enough to put half your attention on the emotion and notice it is there. Imagine an honoured guest was coming for dinner at your house, perhaps someone you had not seen in a long time. Wouldn't you want to clear up and tidy around to make sure you could give them all the attention they deserve? Well, these emotions have been sitting outside your house for a long time and are simply asking to come in from the cold. Incredibly, we find that once we allow ourselves to feel the emotion it will begin to lighten and its frequency will change.

Each emotion is on its own journey back to wholeness but it needs our permission, our attention and our ability to feel it fully.

When attention is on the emotion only, then the thoughts that proliferate in these situations will immediately begin to quiet down. You will know almost immediately that you have hit on something key in your spiritual growth here and in transcending the mind and you will have immediate proof that resisting emotions cause thoughts to multiply and not the other way around (as our mind would like us to believe).

Let's take this one step further by checking in with our real-life examples of student's issues and questions:

Example 1 — Sarah noticed that no matter how much she witnessed the thoughts they still had not disappeared altogether. She felt much more in control again of her mental state but the wish had come to her to be free of these thoughts altogether. She began to notice that when the trigger happened and she was around her step mum Sarah began to not only have many thoughts but she noticed a deep tension or anxiety in her. It was almost as if something inside her was waiting to be triggered. When her step mum was talking about Sarah there would immediately be a huge amount of anger, humiliation and a sense of injustice rising up for Sarah. She felt powerless and noticed a wish to blame her step mum for these feelings.

Sarah realised she could not keep dealing with this issue the same way and so one day when she was at a family gathering her step mum began to talk about her again and was laughing. Sarah flew into a rage inside herself again as usual but this time something collapsed inside her; it was as if she could no longer deny the emotion being felt. She took herself off into the kitchen where she could be alone for a few moments and decided to just simply be angry. She made a decision that no matter how long it took she would just feel the anger and allow it to wash over her completely.

Sarah noticed immediately that thoughts tried to come to get her attention by saying "it is her fault that I feel this way" and many more. In a flash of insight, Sarah realised that if she was blaming someone else then she was not taking responsibility for the anger; in fact she did not even actually know she was angry at her step mum but simply that she felt angry. Yes, of course her step mum seemed to trigger her anger, but now Sarah decided to focus only on the emotion itself. Straight away a tension lifted and Sarah experienced a very strange phenomenon — she felt angry and calm at the same time! It was such a revelation that it was possible to feel both of these at once, that Sarah laughed to herself. Other emotions that came up felt just as strong at first but she knew that as soon as she stopped trying to push the emotion away, it became very light and spread out all over her body. When she resisted it or focused on the thoughts, the anger seemed to be balled up in her gut. But when she relaxed and allowed it, then it spread out all over and began to lighten.

Over the next few weeks Sarah began to embrace any and all emotions she felt on a regular basis and she began to notice a general improvement in her overall sense of well-being. She no longer felt like a ticking time bomb that could go off at any moment. She felt confidence in being able to own her emotions and to release a build-up of emotional energy that previously, she had not even known she was resisting. The more she felt her emotions fully, the quicker they passed and the happier she felt. She recognised it was possible to allow her body to feel an emotion and feel peaceful at the same time although her mind did not believe it! She realised that she only suffered because she had resisted the emotions and not from the emotions themselves.

Example 2 — Michael contemplated his spiritual growth and had begun to appreciate his father much more because of this journey. He had seen that beliefs such as he was destined to end up with all the negative traits of his father, were simply his mind's scare tactics to try to stop him evolving. Michael did still notice though that he had some deep emotions to deal with. When people compared Michael to his father he still felt a lot of shame and humiliation; it brought back unpleasant memories of his childhood too where he had had some embarrassing moments at school. Michael decided to get interested in these emotions because he had made a big breakthrough when he had looked deeply at his father and his thoughts about his father. Maybe it was possible to go deeper into this and find some peace he had not yet experienced.

Over the next few weeks, Michael listed all the negative emotions he felt regularly and he noticed surprisingly that he felt fear, shame and guilt. It was almost like these emotions were ghosts from the past that he had not as yet laid to rest and were coming to get his attention. Michael decided to allow these emotions simply to be felt when they came. It didn't matter to him whether they seemed to be happening for a reason or not. In fact, the more he allowed the emotion to be felt, they seemed to come more frequently at first and often at strange moments. Each time an emotion would come he said a little thank you and imagined his body was a sort of factory for processing emotions. He could feel his body was able to handle any intensity of emotion providing he did not think about it too much. Michael realised he could either feel an emotion or think about the emotion but not both at the same time. In a flash of insight Michael suddenly realised that he was either adding to the emotional pile of stuff to process or reducing it by feeling it and that it was impossible to do both at once.

Over time Michael felt happier, lighter and much more confident knowing that no matter what happened for the rest of his life, he could cope with it. Even intense grief could be handled simply by totally allowing it to happen.

Example 3 — Sally had noticed that over the months she had been working on transcending her mind, that emotions were also a huge part of what she had to look at. It was no longer enough to work on a level of thought only. Sally noticed that the same emotions seemed to be produced by the same trigger event and that sometimes even just thinking about the trigger event caused a barrage of emotion. Even when Sally sat in a peaceful room and simply thought about her neighbour's dog barking all night, Sally felt angry, powerless and frustrated. She became aware that the emotions were the real thing that needed to be looked at because the thoughts were relatively easy now to simply witness. Just like with the thoughts, she found that she had an automatic response to resist any emotion when it came up and the more intense the emotion she felt, the more the urge came to push it away. After realising this Sally felt empowered to simply ignore the urge to push emotions away. She realised she was a grown adult now and not a small child; she could feel safe to allow any emotion to come, last for any duration and pass into nothingness again.

Sally began to consciously feel what she was unable to feel earlier on in her life and she started to relax. The more she felt her emotions the more her body relaxed. The more she relaxed the more confident Sally felt that she could cope in any situation. She felt truly that she had finally come to feel comfortable in her own body and able to face life fully.

Example 4 — David began to notice that most of his issues were related to fear. He feared a lot of things, some of which seemed to be rational but most of them irrational. The more he pondered this, the more obvious it seemed that really what was happening was that a lot of fear had accumulated inside him and he had not been able to feel it. It was as if the fear was asking for attention in the only way it could. It was as if it was creating all these fearful situations to bring attention to itself. Each time David found he did not have enough money or was worried about how he could pay all he needed to that month, he felt that familiar stab of fear deep in his gut. David also immediately noticed an urge to push the fear away or ignore it. It took quite a bit of courage to feel it fully at first but he noticed it became easier each time because he had faced the fear another time. More and more David felt the resistance diminishing and the courage increasing. "Perhaps everyone does not want to feel this too. Perhaps it is like this with everyone?" David asked himself.

The more David allowed himself to feel his fear fully and without condition of how long it should take to go, he felt better and better. He noticed that worrying things still happened financially but more often they would turn around into an unexpected pleasant surprise. He could see the relationship between how much he allowed himself to be available to his emotions and his improving financial situation. If he resisted the emotion when it came up he noticed a tendency to worry and lots of thoughts coming too. Only once he had fully allowed the fear to come, run its course and then to evaporate could he feel a sense of achievement. David realised in one startling moment that he had always been afraid of feeling afraid! He also saw that fear of anything is just fear! He smiled at the simplicity of being able to feel his own emotions for it seemed like the most basic of skills and yet one he was only now learning as an adult.

Example 5 — Jenny had spent a lot of time recently contemplating on her recent breakthroughs. It seemed that the more she investigated her inner world rather than trying to fix or change things in her outer environment, the happier she was. She really felt that she was heading towards a major breakthrough. One day she felt drained and tired, she tried to shake it off but couldn't and a voice inside her urged her to give into it completely. Jenny was not sure what to do but she gave into the urge and felt her physical body feel totally drained. Almost immediately she noticed that her energy began to increase, so she wondered if she could let go even more. As soon as she thought this, she began to feel a lot of fear but also an inner knowing that this too was to be surrendered to. Jenny inwardly said "yes" to this fear and dread and remembered many times she had felt the same way when surrounded by people who seemed to be taking all her energy. In that moment, Jenny saw that it had only ever really been about how completely she was willing to let go and feel whatever she was feeling. However drained she felt was really only due to how much she was resisting her feelings.

Jenny began to see each emotion that she felt was really a question being asked of her; a question that wanted to know how much more she could let go. She had always felt fearful of opening up to others and now Jenny saw this fear was causing the drain on her energy and not the other people. Jenny vowed to stay open no matter what and most importantly, to stay open to whatever her body was feeling. No matter what emotion presented itself, Jenny knew it would only strengthen her energy to open to it and the more she did so the more energy she seemed to feel. Peace, strength and a balanced energy level was now back in her control simply by opening to and welcoming whatever emotion wanted to be felt in each moment.

Conclusion

It is a good idea to make a list of all the emotions that you feel on a regular basis and look at each one in turn. Which emotions are you closed off to? Which do you seem to enjoy in some way? Although this may seem like a strange thing to ask, if we really are honest with ourselves we may be surprised. Perhaps we hate to feel scared and push it away at all costs but we secretly love feeling angry and "venting" or "ranting" at someone. We might hate to feel ashamed and close off to it but we enjoy feeling like a victim on some level too. It is nothing to be ashamed of to notice we enjoy negative emotions on some level; we all do and it is a part of being human.

If we are revelling in a particular emotion we must notice it non-judgementally and simply begin to feel it without thinking about it. Putting attention only on the emotion and not the thoughts about the emotion is key. Feel each emotion when it comes; notice the emotion and welcome it the best you can. Feel as much of it as you can feel and then it will begin to lighten and shift. You will notice that this gives you a sense of confidence and strength in your life which comes from knowing you are able to feel anything that comes.

Remember it is resisting the negative emotions that makes you feel bad, not the emotion itself! You are a human being who is designed to feel. When you fully let yourself do this even with the hardest emotions, you will find your freedom is in your own hands. Don't listen to your mind and fear the emotions.

CHAPTER 8

Stage Four: The Assumptions of Mind

We can see in this stage that all negative emotions are the result of some deeply rooted beliefs about ourselves that we have not wanted to see consciously. These beliefs are thoughts that have been believed so often, that we never question their truth anymore; they come from our environment, our programming and our karma. These beliefs are usually buried deep down within our psyche and manifest themselves in many ways in our lives. We usually have no idea that we believe these thoughts, although we may have noticed these repeating patterns of events happening in our lives that are caused by them. These deep rooted beliefs are often so painful to us because we have come to believe that they are true. The more we have believed them in the past, the more evidence we get that our belief is true and therefore a vicious circle ensues.

We are taught to deal with these beliefs by suppressing them deep down within us or projecting them out onto others with blame mechanisms and other tools.

Once we have transcended the previous stage we will be free of a backlog and burden of heavy negative emotions and will be able to do the research necessary into our own hidden depths to bring these thoughts to the surface. It is important to note that some of these beliefs we may even see consciously are obviously not true and yet it must be accepted that some part of us deeply believes in their validity.

We can begin to find out what these beliefs are by examining how they manifest in our lives. It is important here to ignore the trigger mechanism and thoughts around it and to focus on the emotions that we feel when we are triggered.

We need to look at what message the emotions are trying to tell us. It is as if each emotion that we feel is trying to tell us a story if we will listen. This story IS the belief that is hidden.

For example, we might feel fear of not having enough money and we can keep our attention on the emotion and ask what it is trying to show us. We might begin to see that somewhere deep down we feel that we are not safe.

The key to transcending this stage quickly is to use the emotion to pass the message to you and then focus only on the message.

Transcending the False Ideas in This Stage

Here are the false ideas:

1. These beliefs I have are true and there is nothing I can do about them.
2. I have had these beliefs so long that it will be too painful to look at them.

3. Suppressing or projecting these beliefs makes them go away and I am unaffected by them.

Once we have the list of beliefs we can begin to use a very simple technique of contemplation on their truth. The assumption that our mind has made at some point is that they are true and it has never been questioned since. By believing these thoughts so quickly and automatically we do not even notice that we are no longer questioning them.

The technique works to undo the assumption that they are true and bring them into the light of our awareness. The very moment we begin to question if they are true or not, we are becoming free of their effects and are no longer duty-bound to experience the results of the belief.

To effectively transcend this stage, we must keep our attention on the story from each emotion and not any passing thoughts about the trigger situation. This takes a little effort at first but can be learned easily when we see it is the only way to undo the effects of these beliefs in our lives.

We can begin to disregard any thoughts that are coming up in the moment and keep our attention solely on the story or hidden belief. If we do anything other than this we are only treating the symptoms and not the main "cause" of the issue.

Technique to Undo the Assumptions of The Mind

Our sense of being a separate person is really only a whole collection of thoughts that we repeatedly think until we no longer question their truthfulness. Once we have isolated the beliefs that are buried under the emotions, thoughts and trigger events we can simply notice it and ask if it is actually true. A question such as "Is this really true?" can unlock a whole new shift in our awareness. Normally our mind will simply assume it is true and we will not even notice it is doing that. In this stage we will have become much more conscious of this belief in play, due to having cleared out most of the backlogged emotion that disguises it.

There is nothing wrong with feeling emotions and we will still feel emotions as they arise but here we will know that we need to look deeper, to find the story behind it and question its truth. When we assume that a belief is true we are bound to keep experiencing its effects. When we ask openly and curiously if it is true then we will engage the art of contemplation. As we have said previously, we will feel an experiential shift or a sense of openness that was not there before. We must not stop questioning the truth of these beliefs until we feel this opening. To simply ask the question inside ourselves is not enough; we must give space for an answer to appear in all the forms it wants to do so. These answers will appear as thoughts such as "well of course it is not true", emotional answers such as tears of release and then finally a shift in our consciousness that is beyond thought. When this shift occurs it may feel obvious that the belief is not true and we may question how we ever felt it was.

Let's now look at the examples from our students:

Example 1 — Sarah had written a list of the emotions that she felt after being triggered by her step mum. She noticed that it was really only a few emotions that she felt regularly and it had been the intensity of them that had somehow not allowed her to see that she had been stuck in a pattern with them. Now that she felt much lighter and freer it was easier to notice she felt humiliated, angry and perhaps a little scared of her step mother who seemed to have a great deal of power over her sometimes.

When Sarah sat down and looked at the list she noticed only 3 emotions and she felt empowered. Sarah contemplated each emotion one by one. She sat with a pen and paper and asked the humiliation what it wanted to tell her, even though she felt rather silly doing it. To Sarah's amazement not long after she felt the urge to start writing and she wrote "I am not good enough; I will never be good enough." Sarah felt a deep pull in her solar plexus when she wrote this down, it was as if she was finally exposing something that she had never wanted to see because it was so uncomfortable. She knew that she was onto something though and Sarah remembered thinking this many times throughout her life but it she had never been able to stay aware of it. Somehow it sank back down into the recesses of her mind and she was only now coming to see this had been happening for a long time.

Sarah felt that somehow this time was different because she had unearthed this belief a different way; she had revealed this hidden belief by some investigation and inner work. Writing it down made it harder to forget again and she felt much more able to tackle it. Sarah knew that on the surface of her mind she had many thoughts about how good she was at her job and other things. She had read many self-help books, had learned to meditate and felt quite confident most times. Her self-esteem seemed to be intact and it almost seemed ludicrous that she could still doubt herself at some deep level. The more she looked at this belief, the more of an energetic pull she could feel in her body. Sarah began to question whether this was really only about the fact that a certain frequency of thought had been habitually chosen. Somehow it had become familiar and maybe it mattered very little what the actual belief was. Maybe the process here was simply to reverse the tendency to allow that thought frequency to automatically run through the brain and system.

Encouraged by this Sarah asked herself if this was really true. Was she really not good enough? Immediately thoughts of her achievements in family, academic and career areas of life assured her she was good enough and she felt boosted; however Sarah remembered this was not the goal of the exercise and still held the question in her mind. She sat with the pen and just waited, curious as to what might happen. For a good few minutes nothing seemed to happen but then new thoughts seemed to become available to Sarah. She began to question how she ever had believed this and began to remember her mother feeling the same way many years ago. She remembered incidents from her childhood that had humiliated her in front of her peers. Suddenly a shift occurred inside her and she began to see she had been locked in a vicious circle of believing this was true and therefore having to see the evidence of it over and over again. She began to write that it was not true and it had never been true. She could feel the difference in her words written on the page; they had some sort of different frequency of energy behind them.

Next Sarah moved onto the anger by asking it what it wanted to say. She sat for quite some time and thoughts came to her but she did not feel that she had hit an answer as yet. Suddenly she wrote down "I never get what I want, life isn't fair". Astonished by what she had written Sarah began to contemplate if that was true. The more she looked at those words, the more anger she felt and she also wrote "life is against me and I am not able to change it". Sarah began to cry as she saw that this also had never been true and yet it had appeared to be. She felt an opening and lightening inside her body and the tears came with a sense of relief. No longer would she be bound to play out these beliefs without realising they were affecting her.

Finally she began to look at the fear she felt and she noticed a sense that she wasn't safe. The story here seemed to be "I am not strong enough to protect myself". Again Sarah asked if this was true and waited. After a while she could feel a sense of something shifting within her being and she felt shocked at the realisation that simply questioning the truth and validity of these beliefs was enough to cause a change in her life. She really felt that she had been unconsciously held captive by these beliefs by automatically believing them. It felt like such a freedom to even know she HAD been believing them. How many people are run by similar beliefs their whole life and never even knew about it or that they had a choice?

As she began to notice the trigger event, emotions and thoughts around this Sarah began to make sure she asked the open questions she learned in this stage to ensure she didn't just blindly believe the same thoughts again ever. She began to see evidence of the opposite manifesting in her life; instead of life not seeming fair and it being against her Sarah saw things coming to her right as she needed them. Sarah felt she was perfectly positioned in the flow of events that brought whatever she needed to her. She gained in confidence and ability to say what she wanted and she found it usually helped others too in a way that she could not have foreseen.

Example 2 — Michael had noticed that three emotions came up again and again during his life. Most of the time he felt them when he was with his father or people reminded Michael of his father. He usually felt fear, guilt and shame. Encouraged by the way his life had changed so far with each stage of letting go Michael decided to ask each emotion what it wanted to tell him. He wrote on a piece of paper a list of the three emotions with space to write next to each one. Michael imagined that he was a journalist, waiting for the "news headline" of each emotion. He found it helped to look at the emotion as if it were a living thing. Soon he was rewarded as the fear told him that he did not feel safe being his own man. As Michael looked at this, he realised he had always felt he was not good enough to follow in his dad's shoes. He felt no matter how he tried he would not measure up and that left him vulnerable. He felt unsafe and inadequate. Michael realised his mind had equated being like his dad with being safe and loved. Whenever people pointed out things he did that were like his dad, it only served to remind him that HE didn't feel up to the mark. He questioned the truth of the belief that he was not safe and began to immediately feel lighter. Something inside became open to looking and he saw he had always been safe and all that was happening was that his mind had an ideal set of behaviours and traits it called the end goal. But he was already safe and always had been.

Michael saw the shame was telling him that he had not been good enough at being like his father. It was as though his mind had tied itself in an impossible knot; on one hand he did not want to be like his dad at all and yet somehow, he felt he had to be like him to be safe. When he saw this Michael felt a huge release and saw neither of these beliefs were true. He also noticed the guilt had a similar story behind it of not being good enough. Again, upon questioning this belief, he was no longer bound to experience it and began to feel lighter on all levels. He saw evidence that he was indeed good enough just as he was. People began to change around him even though he had said nothing outwardly of his realisations. Michael finally felt free to appreciate his father for his strengths and also to see how he could grow into his own person.

Example 3 — Sally had distilled down her experience with this trigger event to two main emotions; anger and frustration. Sally looked at the anger and could feel how disempowering it was to her. She wondered what story was underneath it affecting her. After a while, she noticed there was a sense of life being hard, that it was all against her. She noticed that this story had followed her throughout her entire life, although she had only seen it in the issues she was now having. She asked herself if this was true and received a whole bunch of thoughts that told her it wasn't true. Sally knew better than to stop there and kept asking the question. She felt a sense of curiosity about this and felt that she as finally getting to the root of all this. A shift occurred inside Sally and she suddenly felt quite blank for a while and had no thoughts at all. During this time Sally couldn't contemplate anything and felt such peace.

After a while some thoughts began to come back but Sally noticed that it seemed ludicrous that she had ever felt life was hard. Hadn't she also had plenty of evidence that miracles happened too? It was almost as if her unconscious acceptance of this belief had filtered out of her memory all those moments where something good had come to her easily or without effort. The more she asked if this belief was true, the harder it seemed to hold the question inside her. Some part of her was dying, some part of Sally that had bought into these beliefs in the first place was disappearing and she felt such joy at this. Never again would she have to subscribe to these beliefs. She knew she could take an inventory of her life and throw out whichever ones no longer fit her.

Sally also took a look at the feeling of frustration and saw that it came from a deep-seated sense that she could not cope with life; that there was too much to deal with and she was overwhelmed. Sally questioned this again and noticed that even questioning this belief made her feel better. An openness and lightness pervaded her being and she realised she had been overwhelming herself with too many things to do at once. No wonder she felt she could not cope with her life, nobody would be able to, not even a superhero!

Sally noticed an effortless open space within herself that could cope with anything that happened and she vowed to live her life from there. She saw that the frustration had been coming from this belief that she had to have everything sorted out all by herself.

Example 4 — When David learned about this stage of transcending the mind, he could immediately feel that fear had been trying to tell him a story his whole life. He was a little nervous about looking at it but felt boosted by the techniques he was learning. He asked the fear what it wanted to say to him. A deep sense of being unsafe rose to the surface. A voice deep inside him felt small, unsafe and vulnerable. He noticed this feeling had stayed with him his whole life and he wanted to finally bring it into the light.

David began to see how this belief that he was not safe had manifested in his life in so many ways. He could also see that his automatic belief in this story had given it power that it did not have on its own. In fact, in questioning whether it was true, he felt a sense that his whole life had been lived only on the surface of what was possible to experience. He felt as if fear had caused him to back away from truly experiencing the wonder that life had to offer. Now that he could see his belief was reinforcing his experience, David could make a different choice. Each time he noticed he was believing this story again, he simply paused and questioned if it was actually true. Gradually life began to show him evidence that he had always been safe and loved and he could see that this evidence had always been there. It was only his belief in the idea that life was not safe that had coloured all of his experiences, whether he was aware of it or not.

Example 5 — Jenny had noticed that the main emotions she felt were a kind of dread and fear. She asked the dread what it wanted to tell her and was quite surprised at the result. She noticed a thought popping up of "I won't be able to hold onto my energy". It felt as if she was somehow blaming herself at a deep level for the drained feeling she would get. Jenny realised deep down that she had a deep-rooted belief that she should be better than she was.

The moment she saw this belief, Jenny also saw how it had affected her life completely. She began to immediately question if it was actually true; although it appeared that it was. Jenny saw that what played out in her life was a play of appearances, of "seems to be so" and not actually. The more Jenny questioned the truth of this belief the better she felt and at one point Jenny experienced a sense of lightening or opening. A shift was occurring but Jenny vowed to continue to question the assumptions of her mind. She realised it felt better to be open and curious like this, rather than to live in worry of what would befall her next.

Next Jenny tackled the fear and eventually came to see that she believed she was not safe, that other people could hurt her. The belief went deeper than that though. After some patience she saw that she actually believed deep down that other people were bound to hurt her. It was as if somewhere back in her past she had decided on some unconscious level that she was better off alone. She felt that people would only hurt her and make her weak. Jenny was so shocked at this revelation that she sat with it for a while. Suddenly many events of her life seemed to be making sense in a way they never had before and she began to cry at just how much this belief had affected her. She felt a little light-headed and strange for a moment, as if her body could now finally begin to rid itself of the effects of such a toxic belief. She knew from simply seeing this belief she would never be the same again.

Jenny questioned the truth of this belief and felt a shift in her body and her whole way of being. She began to look forward to seeing the evidence of the opposite coming into her life.

Conclusion

In this stage we may be surprised at how the mind actually works. We may even find contradicting sets of beliefs coming up with the investigation that occurs here. We might even find two beliefs that seem completely opposite to each other and yet we have been playing them out somehow all our lives. It is important not to judge ourselves when we see these beliefs and we can instead be grateful that we will no longer be at the effect of them. To be human is to be programmed with these beliefs and most of the population is struggling with similar beliefs at a deep level and don't even know it.

As we do the vital work in this stage, we may begin to see the structures of our mind starting to unravel. It is as if these beliefs have corrupted the normal and healthy functioning of the mind. The mind is burdened by irrational thoughts that have been hidden or projected onto others as they were too painful to look at without the proper tools. When these beliefs first came into our lives we were too young to look at them rationally or logically and they were simply accepted as true. Most of our beliefs may have come from our parents, teachers and other authority figures. However we must be aware that they too were unconsciously carrying them and had no option but to pass them along.

Beliefs such as these are carried down in our DNA and we are totally unaware of them. Other beliefs are picked up as we go through life experience and grow from infancy to adulthood.

Continue with your contemplation, asking if these beliefs are true even when you feel you have had an answer. As we undo the tendency to automatically believe these thoughts, we can experience a never-ending deepening of the opposite of them and life can become quite wonderful.

CHAPTER 9

Stage Five: The Belief in Separation

Before we begin this stage let us remember once again that each time we are ready to move to the next stage of transcending the mind we will notice the same mind pattern coming back. It will appear just as it did before and it may seem as if we have not ever made any progress.

We must remain watchful of thoughts that try to stop us progressing at each stage. These thoughts may be obvious thoughts, such as "there is no point to doing all of this" or they may be more subtle, such as "you have put all this work into transcending this pattern already and here it is again. This technique is not working". Some of the thoughts that try to stop you may even seem to be nothing to do with the skills you are learning in this book. You might have a sudden urge to sleep or feel very tired. You may feel restless as you sit down to read this book or you may have an urge to watch TV or some other distraction. Whilst all of these things are ok to do at normal times, it pays to be aware of when these ideas pop up to distract us from some vital spiritual work.

We may feel motivated to look at our progress in each mind pattern we have and then suddenly we feel overcome by sleepiness for seemingly no good reason.

The next time the same pattern presents itself we must congratulate ourselves that it is now time to move ahead yet again. We must notice that we are about to experience even greater peace, love and joy. If we allow our mind to simply dismiss this as "this stuff is not working — this same mind pattern wouldn't be back again if it was working" then we miss out on one of the greatest spiritual opportunities of our life.

It is precisely because it is working that we are being given another chance to go deeper.

Stage five is one of the key stages in our work. Stage one is where we begin the work and this stage is where the work gets much quicker and easier. In reality each stage after this is simply an extension of this one and we could stop the book after this chapter alone. However each succeeding chapter explains the final process here with more clarity and insight, helping to speed up the disassembly of the mind.

In each previous stage of this book we were working on the assumption that you are separate, alone in the universe; that you are this body and it is all that you are. We were coming from the idea that whatever happens to your body is happening to you and that when it dies, so will you. Now we will move to a much higher viewpoint and begin to make a huge leap in consciousness.

In this stage we will work on a vital assumption of the mind that is at the core of all our suffering as a human. We all believe deep down that we are separate beings. We believe that we are this body and mind and that is all we are. This belief is so pervasive throughout humanity that we never usually stop to question it. If we take a look at how we came to believe this, we can see that it is a normal part of our development. At first we are the formless awareness and when a body appears in it, we naturally become fascinated with it and how it works. We start to entertain thoughts about what we are and what is "mine". We hold onto our body, mind and emotions as "mine" and because of this we fear the end of our body as being the end of us.

Most of us believe so deeply that we are this body, that we are affected by everything that happens in and to the body. In this stage we will look at how to see the truth and how to undo this core assumption. Once we can see that our body is a part of us, as is our mind, then we need not fear the death of the body. Once we know that we are here before and beyond the body, then we can live from a higher place of peace and joy.

All of our problems and suffering stem from this belief that we are separate people. We feel so strongly that we are only this body and that we need things from other people to make us happy. The moment we believe we are alone and isolated from others, then we will feel driven to attain whatever we seem to need to feel happy, safe and secure again. The things we need can be tangible things like money, friends, a good job etc. or it can be intangible things such as enlightenment, respect, a relationship or more.

All of our interactions with others are affected by what we think we need from them. If we can come to see that we are not separate from others at all and that we are all expressions of the Self then we will feel complete. We will know that we

75

need nothing to be happy, peaceful and content. No matter what occurs in our lives we will be at peace.

The very moment we start to question our mind's main assumption that we are a person, alone in time and space, travelling through this lifetime, trying to accumulate as much as possible in the time that we have, we will begin to feel better.

The moment we start to transcend this belief we will see all our problems start to disappear. As amazing as it may seem, it is no longer possible to have a problem when you are not a separate being, but are the Wholeness itself.

Transcending the False Ideas

Here are the false ideas in this stage:

- I am a separate person; I am me.
- I am this mind and body and nothing else.
- Everything that happens to the mind and body are happening to me.

We must simply and consistently begin to question these very deep rooted and core assumptions of our mind. We can do this using the technique we learned in the previous stage of asking "Is this really true?" Again we can ask the question and we will experience the answer on many levels. If we ask ourselves "is it really true that I am a separate person?" we may receive thought answers such as "of course it is true" or "of course it isn't true; I know I am the formless awareness connected to all things". If we stop at these answers, we will not experience a healing and wholeness that comes from living AS the truth and not simply believing in it. If we only believe we are not separate, then we will still experience life as if we are separate.

We must learn to ask the question and to embrace and welcome a lifetime of experiencing the answers to these most vital questions. You will receive many answers and an infinite supply is possible. These will come in the form of thoughts, emotions, sensations, epiphanies and revelations, shifts to a higher level of consciousness, joy, a sense of freedom and much more.

Commit to make your life a living exploration of these questions and you will experience a life that you could have only dreamt of. It starts right now.

Self-Inquiry

This is a vitally important tool which is really extremely simple. It is used to undo assumptions and has been described in some detail in the previous chapter; although it was not called 'Self-Inquiry' there.

Self-Inquiry is simply that we actually look to see if something is true, rather than presuming it is and continuing the mind's assumptions about it. In this case we are actually looking, searching, or scanning ourselves to see if we can find evidence that we are a separate being.

When we simply go along with the assumption that we are separate from everything else, we are adding to an energetic mass of tension within ourselves that has gathered over the years and lifetimes. This tension makes it harder to see the truth or to want to see the truth. However when we stop and actually try to find out what we are, we are beginning to undo this mass of tangled energy. We are breaking free from any confines that we may have had that stop us experiencing happiness and peace.

Each time we actually search for this separate "me" that we think we are (instead of just assuming it is correct) we are going to feel better and better. At first it can be unnerving to realise we are not what we think we are. If we can persist in this looking, searching or scanning we will consistently find that there is no separate person!

Over time and with a willingness to see, we will come to a deep and profound realisation that we have never been separate from anything or anyone and this will allow us to live a much different life. Life can then begin to show us the evidence of our oneness with all of life. Each time we simply believe this thought that we are separate, isolated or alone, we will immediately experience the results of this thought. We will have endless problems with other people, things we seem to need and we will experience life not satisfying our desires. We must choose to check and actually see if we can find this separate person each time we assume it is there, in order to undo this assumption and be free.

Every single human being on this planet that has not already completed this process is convinced they are a separate, unique individual, cut off from everything else and in need of so much to complete themselves and be safe. This is such a fundamental belief in everybody that nobody questions it at all; even though it is the cause of all of the suffering of humanity.

Now that you know this, you have to make a choice to follow that belief and continue to experience life from that level or to take a higher, freer path and be willing to look and see if you have ever been a person. Each time we look, we are confirming more and more that we are not and have never been separate. We are more than this mind and body; we are that in which this mind and body appear and as such we cannot die or suffer at all.

Let us look at our examples from our students. We will see them use self-inquiry to come to the fullest realisations in this stage of our journey.

Example 1 — Sarah began to question if she really was a separate person. She was shocked to find that when she looked for where she was as 'Sarah', she could not find herself! She heard before about a technique called self-inquiry but had never applied it before in this way. Amazingly when she actually stopped and looked, she could not find herself at all. Sarah knew of course, that she must exist because she was looking for herself. But when she looked for where she actually was located she could not find anything concrete. At first she felt afraid of this revelation but as she looked repeatedly, she began to see that it must have always been that way. The whole idea of who she was, what her life was and what she wanted out of it, suddenly seemed to be very strange and dreamlike.

Sarah began to look deeper and deeper into what this meant to her life. She was not this body, she HAD a body that was true, but she was not only this body. What did that mean for her? This and a hundred other questions began to arise for her. She began to see that if she was not a separate individual at all, then all the things she thought had been happening to her were not actually occurring. This was so shocking that it took Sarah some time to get used to this startling revelation.

Sarah saw that she had never been a separate being and realised she could not assume that all of her beliefs, opinions and desires were as valid either. She knew herself to be at a turning point in her journey now, where she could either embrace this revelation fully or turn away from it and go back to suffering. Sarah promised herself that she would not blindly fall asleep to this truth again. She began to contemplate where this left her in her life. Could she be hurt or damaged by someone or something now from this new place? She did not know what she was but she was sure that she was not only this body. She was not a "someone" that things happened to. All around her the world looked exactly the same and yet different. She thought of her step mum and all the issues they have had over the years and felt strangely unaffected by it all. She saw that she could not be affected by anything that anybody said about her; even her step mum. Sarah stayed with this epiphany for quite some time. She felt she had uncovered something vitally important that could slip from her grasp if she did not nurture it. She felt unsure of her future and direction, yet stronger than ever. Could her step mum make her feel any particular way or insult her if she did not even exist as Sarah? This question became vitally important to her and gave her a new found sense of immunity to anything she could say about her. A whole new beginning was occurring for Sarah.

Example 2 — Michael applied self-inquiry to his situation and found that he could not locate himself at all! He began to search and could not find anything concrete. Over and over again he looked and he could not actually seem to find where "Michael" was. He could see his body, his thoughts and he could even see that he was searching but he had no clue as to what he actually was. Michael began to realise that he was not a "someone" that was located "here" or inside his head. He was stunned at first at this profound realisation; he saw that his thoughts were happening inside his head but he could not pinpoint where he actually was. Perhaps he was something more diffuse and of a different quality to those thoughts, emotions and the other things he could observe. Michael spent time contemplating this discovery and wondered how he could have spent his entire lifetime under the assumption that he was located inside this body and that this was all he was.

As he looked more and more he came to see that he could not be like his dad because he could clearly see that he was not like anything at all. What he was Michael could not say but he could see that he was not like anything he could describe or had seen before. All of the experiences he had been through in his life and all the things he had seen had not prepared him for this. Finding out that he was not a thing at all but more like a "no-thing" was strange to discover. He began to see that he could not be like any particular person at all and that he could not even be like he thought himself to be! Michael saw that perhaps he could say that his body moved, talked and behaved in ways that were like his dad but he could not actually say that he was like his dad. He laughed at this revelation as it suddenly seemed very strange to think he could describe himself at all. Michael sat with this discovery for quite some time and he knew that his life would not be the same again. He had been living life from the surface only and it was time to see what was really there.

Example 3 — Sally began to question her assumption that she could be affected by any disturbances or issues. She had come to see over the last few months that usually it was something very different to what she thought was disturbing her anyway. She had begun to see that at the core of all her struggles and suffering, was the idea that she could be harmed or hurt by things in the world. She saw that when she thought she was a person she would always be vulnerable. She would fear the outside world at large or something inside her, like her thoughts or emotions. Sally knew the time had come to dig deeper and to ask what the root of all this struggle was. She wanted to peel back the layers of this problem and find out the cause rather than looking at symptoms. Sally realised that she was the core; she was the root of all that happened to her and that she had never actually investigated what she was. Every time something had happened to her, either positively or negatively, she had never looked once at what she was. Sally saw that she was the central figure in her life and she seemed to be interacting with others but was that true?

Using the self-inquiry tool Sally saw that she was not Sally at all! She was not anything she could describe. Sally was shocked and yet felt free at the same time. If she was not how she had always thought herself to be, then maybe all her issues were not true either. A deep curiosity arose in Sally and an urgency to investigate what she really was came to the surface. Sally looked and found absolutely nothing, nothing at all that she could point to and say "yes that is me". For a while she was stunned and did not know what to do next. She began to get used to the idea that she had never been simply a person, who was living her life and moving through her existence until it came to an end. She began to see that she could not be certain she would come to an end! After all she could not even truly say that her existence had started. Of course she could see that her body had started its existence at a certain point in time and space but not Sally herself. Suddenly she began to see that nothing could affect her at all; even if she imagined it had, it was still not actually so. Life would be very different from now on she decided.

Example 4 — David began to investigate what he actually was. He had always taken for granted that he was David, the person that he and all his family knew. He had always assumed he was a father, a husband and more but had never realised there might be a deeper dimension to his being than that. When David scanned for where he was in reality, he found no evidence at all of a person called "David". He saw that something was present that he had always called himself but it was not as he had thought. He could not find any words to describe it and all he could do was to say what he was not. He could see he was not a person, he wasn't his body because that was something that seemed to be in the same place as he was. He could define himself as intangible and invisible but he could not say what he was.

David became convinced that his fears, doubts and worries were also figments of this imaginary person that he had thought himself to be. If David wasn't actually a real and solid thing then how real were his problems? David saw in a flash that all these issues that he had were like branches growing from a tree of imagination. He saw the root of this tree was this idea that he was a separate being, isolated from all the other people and alone. He could see how his fear would come from such an idea and how deep-rooted that pain must be. David saw that he had been treating the symptoms of an imaginary person and because of this he could never truly find lasting peace this way. He had to stay focused in this new discovery and find out what it meant to his life now. He wanted to know if he could suffer in this place, as this "nothingness" that he found. Had it all simply been a dream in which he had thought himself to be someone growing and experiencing through life?

David also began to see that his needs and wants as a separate person could not also be true because they were based on himself, the central character of his life that did not even exist! Perhaps the gulf between what he needed and what he actually had in life was caused by this belief in being separate. After all, if he was not really separate then what could he actually need and who would provide it? Whose bank account was it anyway that was never full enough?

Example 5 — Jenny began to see that her whole belief that other people could affect her energy and weaken her was dependent solely on the idea that she was a separate being. There had to be some central locus of "Jenny" that existed in one place to be affected. Jenny saw that all of her issues with lacking energy were based around this central idea. It made a lot of sense to Jenny to investigate this most basic of assumptions because this would allow her to solve many problems all at once. She could feel that this was the most important area of focus now and working on the previous levels seemed almost slow and indirect compared to this.

Jenny searched herself to see if she could find a definite answer to where and what she actually was but she could not. She found that all she knew for certain was that she existed; but she could not say what she was. Remembering the issues Jenny suffered with, she began to ask herself if it was true that she could be affected by someone else's energy. She looked and found nothing manifest that she could call herself; more of a presence or a "not yet something solid" nature to herself. As Jenny looked deeper she found nothing other than a vague sense of "I" but nothing that could be affected, hurt or damaged. Of course her body was there and could be hurt by something but Jenny knew this issue around losing her energy would be resolved permanently by looking deeply at what she actually was. Finally, she felt she was dealing with the root of the issue and could resolve it completely.

Conclusion

At this part of our journey we will begin to gain huge benefits from the work we have done so far. It will become easier and faster because whenever we reach this particular stage with any mind pattern, we will be working on ALL our mind patterns simultaneously. All of our mind noise is being generated from this one belief. That may sound too simple to be true but we can verify this if we are willing to look a little deeper. Each time we say "I need..." or "I don't have.." or "I want..." we will see that it involves this central character in our lives that we believe to be very real and solid.

Even when we have a problem with another person, rather than ourselves, that other person is still affecting "me" or "my life". If we can digest this deeply within our being, we will come to see that all our issues can be resolved with this master key that we have been given in this stage. We may feel as though we have been working one particular mind pattern all the way back to its most basic roots. If we are open to see it, we will realise most profoundly that even in stage one we were actually working on this stage.

There has only ever been one problem in our lives. There has only ever been one issue to resolve. All other seeming problems are simply this one dressed up to look like something else and to throw you off the path. In the previous stages of this process we learned that our mind does not like to change anything because it fears our destruction. Notice that it has tried to camouflage this main belief in as many different ways as it can. Now we can see that these are simply ways to spend time fixing endless problems and that our mind will simply make more problems for this "me" to have. It is an endless cycle. The quick and easy way out is to work at the root and fix all issues at once.

It really is this easy and simple. It takes time to see this deeply and to learn to stay focused here and not be diverted again.

CHAPTER 10

Stage Six: The Belief in Otherness

In this stage we are going to look deeper into what it means to be formless. For many of us we may have used self-inquiry to effectively eliminate any tendencies to think of ourselves still as a thing, an object or something perceivable. We may have come to understand that we are formless and beyond being damaged, ageless and timeless; but we may not have realised the full implications of what it means to be formless.

We can still hold other people, events and things we seem to need as being "other" than us. For this stage of the process to be fully understood and assimilated, we must come to see that there is nothing other than us.

If you are formless and cannot find an end to yourself when you look, then you must be all that exists. You are the emptiness or nothingness from which all forms arise and are made out of.

At this point I could instruct you to stop and deeply contemplate this and you should, however this would not eliminate what will happen in this next stage. Let us look closer at what is next in this disassembly process that we are applying to our mind and see if we can understand why.

You are the source of all that exists and you are all that ever has existed, exists right now and could exist in the future. What you are is the formlessness which contains all possibilities of what may manifest and all that has manifested into actuality.

As you read, apply and comprehend this you will come to feel a deep sense of peace and completion. It will feel as if you are living in a place that is involved in the world of people, events and things but is also somehow protected and immune from the dramas of the world. Every once in a while you will come across something that seems to make you suffer again but this is not what is actually happening. It is important that you take a moment to read and fully contemplate the following statement:

Each time you feel you are suffering again, you must look and find out what is being shown to you. Life is trying to show you what you have left out of your Allness. You are all of the unmanifest formlessness and the manifest too. If there is anything that you have left out of that, then you will feel a sense of division inside yourself because there will seem to be "me and other". If you are all of it then there is nothing other than you. The body that wrote this book is you, the students quoted in this book are you, Christ is you, Stalin was you. We could quote endless examples but we must come to see that all animate and inanimate things are you.

This book came out of you, written by you, to help you see your Allness. You are all of it.

We must come to accept all of creation as us, including the highest and lowest acts of humanity, in a non-judgemental and non-personal way. I am not asking you to take personal responsibility for all that has gone wrong in the universe. If you do, then you have not understood the previous stage deeply enough. I am also not asking you to feel proud of all the positive achievements of the universe so far, because this would also be taking things personally as a separate self.

You must come to see that no matter how this formlessness expresses itself, it is you. You are expressing yourself in every conceivable way you can and will continue to do so without end. Infinite expressions are possible and the only thing you can know is that you will never express yourself the same way twice. So, you can come to see that All is you and you are All of this. If you feel a struggle within you it is because you are reverting to old thought patterns around a particular person, event or emotion and this is causing you to separate yourself from it. Suddenly there is "other than you".

Let's look at the false ideas in this stage.

<u>Transcending the False Ideas</u>:

- I am formless but other people, places, events and things are still real and separate, there is an end to my formlessness. Everything else is other than me.
- The manifest is different from the unmanifest and I am unmanifest. The manifest forms in the universe are "other" than me.

The second false belief may not be immediately noticeable but we all have a tendency to define ourselves. The moment we define what we are we automatically exclude anything that does not fit within that definition. If we know that we want the security of knowing what we are, then we can begin to cease defining ourselves in thought, image or ideas. Words such as "unmanifest" and "manifest" suggest mental images that our minds can hold onto. There truly is no word to describe what you are. The best our mind can do is to try to combine manifest and unmanifest and imagine what that looks like.

You will know that this second belief has been transcended when you no longer see something as manifest, you no longer notice the coming and going of things. It all begins to feel the same with no separate witness watching the play of the manifest world.

Our role now is to take an inventory of our life and to notice where we are still holding things as "other" than us. It may be a certain person that we go into a divided state with or a lack of something, such as money. When we go into division, instead of being the One Formlessness, we feel we are one AND the money, time or peace that we feel we need. There are immediately two things; us and what we need and so we are in effect saying "I am all things except this thing that I need". If we had already included it in our Oneness, then we would not feel we need it nor would we notice a lack of it in our experience.

Our life will be showing us, if we are willing to see, what needs to be taken into and included in our wholeness. We must be willing to see what we are unconsciously excluding to be able to stay as the Truth of who we are. If we are not willing to see we will fall asleep again, live as if we are separate and begin to suffer again.

Formlessness has no boundary, no end point and it must go on forever. You must go on forever, you are infinite and all-pervading and so there can be nothing that exists that is other than you.

Let's look at our examples from our students to help clarify this stage:

Example 1 — Sarah began to see that although she knew herself to be without form and not separate, she had not allowed that knowledge to fully penetrate her entire life. When she thought about or interacted with her step mum she felt a sense of division arise inside herself. Sarah realised that her step mum was also not a real person. "Step mum" was just a name for another human body that was appearing in the formlessness, in the formlessness that was Sarah.

Sarah contemplated this for some time and she realised that she had been holding her step mum outside of her being and not including her in it. Sarah noticed a part of her mind that was very resistant to including this woman as a part of her. It seemed much easier to accept that the Buddha, Mother Teresa and all of her heroes were the same as her; the One formlessness expressing itself as all these forms. She felt that she was being presented with a big challenge or test. Could she find it within herself to admit that another aspect of herself which appeared as her step mum could be cruel and vindictive and all the things Sarah had tried to move away from? This seemed to stop Sarah for quite some time as the unwillingness grew to pass this test. Somewhere deep down she knew that it was a test most people would not pass. Everyone wanted to admit that they were Christ or Krishna but not Hitler or any of the other people society loved to hate or blame.

Sarah contemplated again and asked if it was really true that this was difficult to accept. She did not know how she would do it but she knew she must. Suddenly it seemed obvious to Sarah that it made no actual difference to her whether she admitted her step mum was just another unique expression of what she was; it did not change anything in actuality. All that would happen is that if Sarah did not embrace this, she would divide herself into two beings again and suffer. Her step mum had always been a part of her and Sarah had always been formless. Nothing was actually changing except now Sarah knew the truth of her being.

With this realisation it seemed pointless to deny the truth and Sarah knew by admitting it she would no longer be affected by anything her step mum said. She felt a sense of compassion for her step mother that she had not reached before and began to feel that she would like to help her. When she was around her step mum Sarah noticed that she must be vibrationally mis-matched with her step mum now as they didn't seem to be able to stay in the same room for long. How ironic it seemed to be that the more she loved and accepted her step mum, the less interaction with her she seemed to have. Some energetic barrier seemed to be protecting Sarah from any further issues with her.

In the end Sarah came to see that it was her belief in being separate from her step mum that was actually keeping her stuck in the current cycle. Seeing her and getting upset at the things she said was reinforcing the belief that they were separate beings all over again.

<u>Example 2</u> — Michael pondered the issues deeply and came to see that he was still holding his father as a person, a separate individual who was different to himself. He realised

that his father must also be himself too, appearing as a different expression but from the same formless source as him.

Michael and his dad were but two bodies appearing in the One source of all that is and so he saw he could not be like his dad at all. Michael saw he could not also be unlike his dad. These ideas both fell away as being ridiculous when he saw there was only one being in the universe. The most that Michael felt he could say was that this body of his had expressed some of the genetic traits passed on from his father's DNA. He could not be like or unlike him however because that meant two beings would have to exist and that was impossible.

Michael understood finally that the idea that they were two beings was all that had ever upset him, his mind had told him it was because he was being compared to his dad but Michael could see the truth. From his wholeness Michael could see what his mind could not see; there was only this one being and the idea that there could be two beings was so false that it caused him to suffer when he believed it. This was and always had been the only real issue in his life.

Example 3 — Sally began to really contemplate what it meant to be formless. She saw that she didn't have any location at all and that must mean that she is everywhere. This seemed a strange revelation to her at first but it began to feel more obvious as she looked at it more and more. A strange feeling occurred within her body when she heard the dogs barking down the street and Sally noticed a tension or anxiety inside her body. Sally recognised that when she self-inquired this tension left her body immediately and when she focused back on thoughts about the dog barking it returned just as quickly. Some things in her life seemed to cause an even deeper sense of tension and tightness in her body.

Sally realised that her body had an innate intelligence of its own in each cell and it was responding to whatever she was thinking about or focusing on. When she used the self-inquiry technique to confirm again her formlessness and lack of boundaries, she felt deeply relaxed and at peace. Contrary to that when she thought of something that upset her, the tension came back. Her body was telling her moment by moment, what caused her to go into division within herself! Sally recognised this and was amazed at the simple yet profound intelligent feedback her body was giving her right now. She began to notice that her body had always been giving her this feedback but she had not known.

For the rest of her life, Sally would not need to get lost in a dream for very long because her body would most certainly tell her when she was holding something or someone separately. Realisation dawned on Sally that the dog itself, its barking, her reaction to it internally and her acceptance of it, were all aspects of herself appearing as emotions, thoughts, dogs, noises and much more. Sally saw cascading out of her a range of infinite ways she could express herself. She was the dog as much as she was Sally and that gave her great peace. The dog's body was just doing what it was supposed to by barking, just as her body was doing exactly what it was supposed to.

Sally thanked her body silently for all the help it had given her to come to this realisation and pondered if in fact, this was the reason she had this body. It suddenly seemed obvious that without a human body she could never know when she was dividing herself into two beings in her imagination.

It was impossible to actually split herself, she had never actually been separate to anything else in the universe but she could sure have a realistic experience of suffering if she believed she was separate to the dogs and anything else. With this understanding a great deal of tension left Sally once and for all. She was safe now, on the home stretch, and all she had to do was to pay attention to her body and allow it to tell her whether she was believing in separation or living as the Oneness.

Example 4 — David had progressed very far in his research into his mind and how it worked. He felt he was very close to a big shift in his consciousness. He noted that although he had seen many times that he was formless, more like space than person, he still seemed to need money as much as he had done before. Most times the money he needed came much faster and easier to him but he realised he must be missing some vital realisation.

David contemplated this and began to see that he was still separating himself in his mind into a person who needed money. He saw in a flash that this was two things; himself and the money. David realised he must be the money he was trying to get and that any attempt to attract it or earn it, would only drive it away by forcing himself into division with it. With a smile David saw that he must know himself to be all of it and he could no longer believe that he needed anything. Of course his body would still go to work and earn his wages but he would not ever need anything again. He had been trying to receive something that was already here, he had been trying to get more money and that money was what he was. Money was just another way he had appeared in the universe and if he was infinite and present in all forms, then he must also be the money he needed.

A shift occurred in David's consciousness as he realised he had actually never needed anything at all. The sense of need and desire had only come because he had somehow convinced himself that he was a separate person who needed resources to survive. David was being asked to live from a higher place now and he could see that each time he needed something, it would serve as a reminder that his thinking had dropped to this lower place of separation again.

Example 5 — Jenny had begun to see that the whole reason she suffered and struggled with her energy was because of this idea of otherness. Believing in herself to be separate, automatically made everything else as "other than me" and she could see this was associated somewhere deep in her mind as dangerous or to be avoided. Jenny saw that she could either spend the rest of her life trying to balance her energy and protect it from other people, places and events that seemed to affect her; or she could deeply internalise the reality that there is nothing other than her. If indeed she was formless (which she was coming to accept and see more easily) then she must be everywhere. Formlessness cannot have any edges and that left her with only one conclusion; she was all of it and there actually were no others to affect her.

Within her mind something reared up to resist this knowledge because there would be a profound shift in consciousness upon knowing this deeply and nothing would be the same. Jenny saw that she feared this leap in consciousness because it was unknown to her. She could see that her only issue had been this sense of otherness. If she allowed this sense of otherness to dissolve she would have no issues ever again. Some part of Jenny was excited about this beyond measure and yet another part of her was very afraid. Jenny decided to look at why there was fear and she realised that she believed she would not be herself after this leap in consciousness; that some vital part of her would be lost forever. Jenny decided to dive deeper into this fear and asked if it was actually true that she would lose something vital and valuable upon realising her true nature and living as that.

Jenny pondered this question for quite a few days and seemed at first to get no answers at all but then something quite amazing happened. Jenny saw clearly that she had always been herself, she had always been the Self. Coming to finally live as that 100% of the time would not actually change anything at all. She had always been this true Self that she saw now included everything and obliterated all sense of otherness. How could she lose anything if she was not actually changing at all? All that would happen from this level of consciousness would be that her experiences would be much more pleasant. She saw that she was being asked to make a choice whether to live in fear or live in truth.

This revelation gave her a renewed sense of confidence and purpose. She began to react and respond to everything and everyone in her life as if they were another aspect of her. She realised that some part of her had been addicted to the drama of having these issues. Instead of reacting to others she found a sense of growing peace and a silence that was always present in the background. It was as if the belief that there were others that affected her had been like a thorn in her side and had caused her mind to constantly react over and over again in the same old way. Now something could rest deep inside herself. Whilst it sometimes took a little conscious effort to remember that whatever was presenting itself to her was Jenny in another form, the rewards were more than worth it!

Conclusion

This stage of the process is really an extension of the previous stage and is really asking you to make a decision to live from the truth of yourself that you have seen. If we continue to interact with life from the viewpoint of being a separate person interacting and reacting with others, then we will come to see that we are living in a very small way. It is our chance now to live from the fullness of all that is possible for us. We can move about through life knowing that no matter what happens or who we meet for the rest of our lives, we will be meeting ourselves. It is very different to live from and as this truth but it is profoundly rewarding. More practically, it helps us to navigate through all of life with its challenges and unexpected changes.

CHAPTER 11

Stage Seven: The Belief in Becoming the Allness

This stage is simple to understand but it may need some time for the impact of it to fully blossom in your consciousness.

Once we have seen deeply that we are the formless awareness and that everything else is too, then our outlook on life begins to change. We may find that we are less and less tolerant of the places in our life that we are still seeing from illusion. We may find that we seem to oscillate between knowing we are the formless presence and the other extreme of feeling like we are a separate person.

We may set about eradicating those areas of illusion from our life and may feel that we are making progress for a while. Most of us will come to see though that things we thought we had transcended even at this level, keep coming back again and we seem to suffer.

To transcend this stage we must come to see that we are not actually transcending the separate sense of self at all. This is what our mind will want us to believe but we must continue to be the Truth.

There never was any separate person called "me" and as such there is no work to do in order to eliminate this separate person. It is an illusion that has no existence in reality. What we have called the separate "me" is simply a collection of thoughts about being a separate person. When these thoughts are believed we have the experience of being "someone".

The last place that this separate sense of self will seem to hide is as someone who is transcending separateness more and more and spending less and less time in illusion. We can come to believe quite easily that we are making progress, that we are evolving more into living as the Truth. We can feel like we are eradicating the sense of being someone and only being the Self.

The Self is all that ever was, is and will be. There never was any false personal self. You never have been separate.

Any belief that it takes time to rid yourself of illusion is simply not true. It takes no time for light to illuminate the darkness when you switch on the light.

Illusion is not real, it has no existence and therefore it takes no time at all to get rid of illusion.

We will understand this more when we look at the false idea in this stage:

Transcending the False Ideas:

1 — I have to get rid of all that is untrue within my being. I must transcend wherever I am still believing in separateness.

2 — It takes time to fully live as the Truth, I may have seen what I am clearly but to live as that in all areas of my life takes time. I can do something that will make the separateness go away.

We must be sure to remind ourselves that there is no work to do now from this place. It is a matter of vigilance only from this point on. Our mind will try to find a way to activate a new sense of self as a separate person and so we will need to watch we are not allowing that on some level. If there is time needed in this stage, it is because we must remind ourselves that separateness was never true until it is no longer necessary. It will be easy to see where we are still believing in time and having to transcend something because that area of our life will not be flowing as well as all other areas.

Finally we come to see that there is no time, no process, no transcendence or letting go of anything. There is no need for practice to "stay as the Self" as all is the Self. There is only the Allness that encompasses all illusion too. It is all the Self.

At this point the remainder of the dysfunctional mind will lose its grip and there will be great peace, love and joy.

Let's look at the examples from our students to help illustrate this stage:

Example 1 — Sarah began to realise she had never been separate from her step mum. She saw with increasing clarity that viewing her step mum as separate had inadvertently caused her to be viewed as something hostile. Sarah began to see that if she maintained her vision from the true place, her step mum would be no threat to her; nor could Sarah suffer from anything she said.

Sarah realised she had a tendency to still think of her as being separate to her step mum. As this realisation came Sarah heard a thought pass through her mind saying "it is going to take a while to change my point of view" but she knew that this was a trap. She did not want to believe it would take a while because it was simply not true. At some point it must have taken a while to begin to think of everyone else as being other than her. Now she was seeing truly it took no time at all to reverse it.

Each time Sarah had a similar thought to this one, she would simply remind herself that it had never been true. Sarah could not suffer now and she knew all her suffering had been self-inflicted in a way. Now she could see everyone and everything as being another aspect of herself; she was manifesting herself in so many different forms and it was amazing to see.

Sarah noticed she would perhaps still not choose to spend too much time with her step mum. When she was with her, Sarah felt at ease and she knew that nothing could hurt her now. She was all that there was, is and ever will be.

Example 2 — Michael had seen with some clarity that what he had always thought of as his father, was another body appearing in himself. He saw that all bodies appeared in him and he was in all bodies. Both of those statements seemed to feel very true. He knew that it seemed absurd now to try to compare himself to someone or something because that would mean they were other than him.

Michael saw that the idea of "father" and "mother" were simply concepts that we had all been taught to believe in.

The "father" and "mother" would also not exist without the child being born. They would just be human bodies.

Michael realised that on the surface of his life, the way that the manifest aspect of the Self moved, he would always have a family and ties to them emotionally. Also on a much deeper level, he knew that all of humanity was his real family. He knew that to view his mother, father and siblings as special and more meaningful to him than all the rest, had been the cause of his suffering all along. The idea that a human being could love 7 billion other humans with the same depth of feeling was strange to Michael at first but he saw he was only returning to live in the natural state. In the end Michael saw that he could not even love 7 billion humans because there was only the One Being appearing as many.

As this sunk deeper into Michael's awareness it began to pervade everything he did. He could speak to the postman or anyone else with the same respect and patience as he would have for his father. He realised that respect, patience and kindness were actually forms of expressing love that were acceptable to society. Although he applied different rules for expressing love to his children, his father, his siblings and his cat, he could see that by knowing what everyone else really was he would always be radiating love to them. He found it impossible to exclude anyone from this love that encompassed all of life.

Example 3 — Sally had seen already that she had been disturbed by the dog barking in the neighbour's house only because she would think about it. She came to see that only when she thought about the dog did it actually exist in her mind. A thought passed through her head that said "dog" and suddenly a dog had appeared. With a loud laugh Sally realised how strange it sounded that she had just made a dog appear. She knew that the dog itself was not thinking about her and saying "Sally". "Perhaps animals are so at ease because they have no ability to separate themselves from everything else in thought" Sally realise. "Dog" did not actually exist anywhere but inside her head at the exact moment of the thought. Sally realised that "Sally" also did not exist as an entity unless she was thinking of it too.

The most profound revelation of all was suddenly very obvious to Sally. She saw immediately and clearly that it is only possible to separate ourselves from everything in our imagination; that even if we are thinking about "other" people, animals or places that does not actually make them separate. Sally laughed out loud when she saw that human beings lived in a virtual world of imagination, where lots of things and people and events happened that were not actually real. She saw that all that was occurring in reality, was that shapes were rising and changing in the manifest aspect of herself; like waves forming on the ocean, cresting for a while and then dissipating. How strange, Sally thought, that we try to separate everything and then give it a name for its duration of existence. She could somehow imagine how a dog or cat might see the world now. How simple and yet beautiful. How strange that human beings were, in effect, trying to name all the waves that rose to the surface! Not only that but all humans had favourite waves and tried to hold on to them.

Example 4 — David's contemplations had brought him to see that there never was such a thing as money. He realised that what he had called money was simply the Self manifesting as notes, coins and numbers on a bank account screen. The idea of giving and receiving suddenly seemed to be very strange to him. He had spent so much time before he knew about this trying to receive money. He had followed a lot of "spiritual" people and tried to transcend the need for physical wealth and abundance. He had tried many things but they all seemed to make it worse for himself and now he could see why. Anything that David did to try to "allow" or "receive" money would simply cause an imaginary separation in his energy that had to push money away from him. There was nobody to work, nothing to earn and nobody to receive it! Who would his paycheque go to anyway? David saw that this was all just numbers swirling around from one account to another anyway.

David decided he would go to work because he wanted to; not because he needed to earn money. Those ideas had kept him in a relative lack of abundance. In fact he had been living in lack so consistently due to his ideas about money being real, that he had clearly seen he had an abundance of lack in his life! He laughed at this revelation — anything he believed to be true he would receive in abundance and he had been receiving a lot of lack! David saw that there was only the Self and paper notes and coins were just one of an infinite number of ways it can show itself. David felt himself relaxing and decided it was time for an abundance of abundance to show up instead. He saw that as the Allness itself, no lack was actually possible; there is no void or gap in the Allness (or else it would not be All).

David went to work to have fun and to serve the "other" people he saw around him. He saw that they very clearly still believed in lack and in "otherness" but he knew his energy would be helping them in some way. He lived his life from a place of wholeness and completion and let go of old ideas about lack and needing. His life felt complete and he was at peace no matter what experience he was having.

Example 5 — Jenny had spent a lot of time pondering how she could have ever come to see herself as isolated from all other human beings. It seemed strange now to think that anything could be separate in this great Being that is all of this. She saw how quickly human thinking can create strife and trouble where there really is none.

In her own life she saw that the idea of separation had held so much fear for herself that she had come to vibrate that all others were harmful to her energy. How she had lived with such a belief for so long and managed to survive was evidence to Jenny that the real strength of the Self was absolute. Nothing could harm the formless Self although her belief that it was possible had given her a convincing experience of it.

Jenny realised that she had always been absolutely fine and that she had never been out of balance or even in balance with others. It seemed to her that she had simply let her imagination run wild and because everyone else also believed they were separate, there was nobody to tell her otherwise. Now she knew that it had never been true and it felt good.

Jenny noticed that if she began to believe in time or a process, her body would immediately let her know; she would feel the familiar drain again. Sometimes when she was with her husband or children she had a tendency to still think of them as separate to her and she was reminded quickly by her energy levels dropping. It didn't matter to Jenny because she was amazed at how quickly she was back to abundant energy. All she had to do was to remember that she had never been a person, she never had "other" people around her and that there could not actually be any drain on her energy because there was nobody to drain it from her.

Jenny was astounded at how quickly her energy returned the moment she remembered the truth again. She felt grateful that she would not be able to fall 'asleep' again and suffer for very long before her body let her know what was happening. She smiled as she realised that this was what was happening to people all around her each time they yawned, complained of being tired or said that they had not had enough sleep last night. They just did not know the true cause of their fatigue was their belief in themselves and others.

CHAPTER 12

Conclusion

Each mind pattern that you notice can now be seen as a key to total freedom and an end to suffering. You are being given a chance each time you suffer to use it and turn it around into total transcendence. As we have said before, each time you peel back another layer of the mind you gain back more of your energy and spiritual power to speed the rest of the process. It need not take that long to come to silence, stillness and peace if you are committed to this process.

All the tools you need are here and now that you are reaching the end of the book, I would urge you to take a moment and make a list of the mind patterns you still have. Try to identify which stage you feel you are at with each one. Be aware that you may be at stage one with some of them and also at an advanced place with another one. There is no rule that says you must be on stage three with all the mind patterns you have.

There will be some that are hard to spot and understand and perhaps if we did not have the trigger event still going on in our lives, we might not see that we are still believing in separation somewhere. All of us have patterns that are easy to see and we all have some that are well-hidden. This is normal and it does not mean you are not making progress.

If you reach the final stage with any pattern, you may feel an urge to stop working on all the other ones. Simply focus your attention on the fact that separation was never true and there is nothing that can harm you, nothing that you may need and you can never die because you are formless and immortal. There is no correct way to transcend the mind that works for all of us but there is the correct way for you. Go with your instinct and ask for help. Prayer and contemplation help us to see where we are missing vital pieces of information too. Help will come to you from many sources when you need it.

A Final Note

At each stage of this journey you will feel more peace, love and joy. There is no rule that says you must completely transcend the mind. If you want to stop at any point that is totally okay. This book is written as guidance for those whose heart will not allow them to rest until they have absolute freedom from mind and suffering is no longer possible. However, you will know what is right for you. Go as far as you want to go; just be sure you have not stopped because mind is distracting you.

I wish you many blessings and peace. Enjoy the journey and always remember you are already free, liberation is already what you are.

Om

Om

Om

Namaste.

APPENDIX

Summary of Common Names for the Noumenon

Below are some of the ways the Noumenon has been described in other teachings. For each set of terms there are two names. Reading through the list may help to awaken a recognition in you as you read and at certain times along the way different sets of terms may be more appealing than others.

They are all names for That Which Has No Name. Don't get attached to any name; look at what the name points to.

NOUMENON	PHENOMENA
Oneness	many
Allness	separation
Empty Mind	full mind
Unity	multiplicity
Silent Mind	noisy mind
Non-Duality	duality

"I" as Consciousness	"I" as a person
Nothingness	somethingness
Awakeness	sleep/dream
Consciousness	unconsciousness
Silence	sound
Subjectivity	object
Being	being someone/ something
Stillness	movement
Presence	person
God	ego
Truth	falsehood
Formless	form
Reality	illusion
Knowingness	knowing about
Awareness	perception
Context	content
Infinite Field	finite being
Timeless	duration

If you would like more information about Helen Hamilton, her live Satsangs, silent retreats and classes please contact us:

Our website is www.helenhamilton.org

Find us on facebook by searching @satsangwithhelenhamilton

Search for us on YouTube at "satsang with helen hamilton"

Email us at evolutionofspirit@gmail.com

Made in the USA
Las Vegas, NV
23 March 2021

20025647R00073